— Mastering the Art of —

CARVING MELON CENTERPIECES

—Lonnie T. Lynch—

Boca Raton, Florida

— Illustrated by Susan Pribish —

Including:

- *Easy Step-by-Step Instructions*
- *Over 30 Melon Designs for Your Use*
- *Tool Usage Section*
- *Stencil Usage Section*
   and More…

L. T. LYNCH • Culinary Marketing • Press Books are available at quantity discounts when used to promote or sell their products. To place an order, or for information, please write to:

L. T. LYNCH • Culinary Marketing •
9850 Sandalfoot Blvd; Suite #226
Boca Raton, Florida 33428

• **Lonnie T. Lynch** •
– *Culinary Marketing* –

Publishing Venture

Published in the United States by
L. T. LYNCH • Culinary Marketing •
Library of Congress cataloging in process.

ISBN 0-9629277-1-6

— Acknowledgments —

To my mother, Joyce D. Agee, I would like to give special thanks. Also, to Patricia Bailey a special thank you!

Special Recognition to —

Bob Barry, my good friend always. I could not have completed these projects if not for your valuable help and guidance.

American Culinary Federation

Florida Culinary Institute

I wish to thank everyone for their support on my first book, "Carving Watermelon Centerpieces".

© Copyright 1995, Lonnie T. Lynch

All Rights Reserved

9850 Sandalfoot Boulevard, Suite #226
Boca Raton, Florida 33428

— Table of Contents —

Acknowledgments 3
Introduction 7
Melon Types 9
    Grades 9
    Care 9
    Tips 9
    Variety 9
Melon Types, continued 10
    Availability 10
    Tips 10
Stencil Usage Section 11-12
    X-Acto Knife 12
    Grid Enlargement and Reduction 13
Tool Usage Section 15
    Paring Knife 15
    V-Tool 15
    Melon Baller 15
    Channel Knife 15
Illustrations of above tools in use 16-17
Decorating Usage Section 18
    Support and Background Materials 18
Hints & Tips 19
Photo Section 20-24

PATTERN STENCIL SECTION 25

    Anchor and Wreath 26
    Angelfish with Seaweed 28
    Bird of Paradise 30
    Cantaloupe Turtle 32
    Christmas Dove Ornament 34
    Christmas Reindeer 36
    Christmas Tree 38
    Classic Swan 40

Table of Contents

Dolphin	42
Dolphins, Three Jumping	44
Dove	46
Eagle	48
Fourth of July Liberty Bell	50
Honeydew Kissing Doves	52
Honeydew Vase with Cantaloupe Flower	54
I Love You	56
Melon Vase Carvings	58
Palm Tree	60
Paradise Fish	62
Quarter Moon	64
Sailfish	66
St. Patrick's Shamrock with Pot O' Gold	68
Scallop Shell and Palm Tree	70
Seahorse with Seaweed	72
Seal with Ball	74
Southwestern Cactus Carving	76
Southwestern Coyote Carving	78
Star of David	80
Swordfish with Banners	82
Tropical Bird	84
Vase	86
Honeydew Dragon	88
Swan I	92
Swan II	95
Letters, #s, & Marks	99
Melon Recipes	105

Order Forms and Notes's Area in Back

— Introduction —

"WELCOME TO THE WORLD OF CULINARY ARTS"

A hundred years ago Escoffier said, *"Faite Simple,"* make it simple and that is what I've attempted to do for you.

ART (*art*) n. The use of imagination to make things of aesthetic significance; The technique involved; The theory involved; Objects made by creative people.

After having created hundreds of watermelon, melon and ice carving centerpiece displays, I decided to create a book titled **"Mastering the Art of Watermelon Centerpieces"**. I was overwhelmed with the response, and the request for a melon book. I then set out to create a book with new techniques and skills, to further simplify elaborate centerpieces.

My second book in this series of culinary art is titled, **"Mastering the Art of Carving Melon Centerpieces"**. In this book, I will share with you professional methods and culinary know-how accumulated over the years, to help set the theme for many different types of holidays, special functions and parties for all to enjoy.

Culinary arts can be fun! It is even more fun when you enter your kitchen with *confidence* and with the knowledge that you know exactly what to do and how to do it. **"Mastering the Art of Melon Centerpieces"**, will give you that *confidence*. Work hard, work carefully and above all *enjoy* what *you* do.

—Mastering the Art of—
Carving Tallow Centerpieces

—Mastering the Art of—
Carving Watermelon Centerpieces

— Melon Types —

Grades —

Grades for melons are: U.S. Fancy; U.S. No. 1 and U.S. No. 2. The grades conform to the U.S. Department of Agriculture's policy of establishing uniform grade names for fresh fruits and vegetables.

Care —

At temperatures of 32° - 50° Fahrenheit, melons are subject to chill injury. After one week at 32° F., they will develop an off-flavor and become pitted. At 32° to 50° F., they lose color. At higher temperatures, they decay.

Holding melons at room temperature can improve flavor and coloring.

The best way to determine flavor and maturity is by plugging. Good, ripe, melons are firm, perfectly shaped and fresh looking.

Melons should not be mealy or water soaked.

Tips —

For creating exquisite and satisfying carvings, select fruits not only according to taste, but also according to the visual elements of size, proportion, color and texture — both inside and out. Melons should not be bruised, or odd-shaped and should have no decay or soft spots.

Varieties —

Honeydew: Size should be six inches or more in diameter. Light green flesh, juicy and with a fine texture. Color of skin should be greenish white, with light yellowish streaks.

Cantaloupe: Size should be five inches or more in diameter. Yellowish, not green skin. Salmon, to orange colored flesh should be moderately sweet.

Casaba: Choose four to seven pound melons. Color of skin should be golden yellow, with white flesh.

Juan Canary: An oblong melon. Color of skin should be bright yellow. The flesh is sweet and white, with a pinkish color around the seeds.

Santa Claus or "Christmas": These melons weigh ten pounds or more. Flesh is pale green, sweet and mild.

Crenshaw: Normally 7 to 9 pounds. Flesh is a pinkish, salmon color, tangy and moderately sweet.

Melon types continued on next page:

— Melons, continued —

Melon types continued —
   Orange Flesh Melon: A cross between a honeydew and a cantaloupe.
   Other Varieties,   *Sharly, Spanish, Persia, Ogde, Galia, Lavon and Honeyball.*

Availability —
March through October is the heaviest volume.

Tips —
As you, the artist, start to practice *"Mastering the Art of Carving Melon Centerpieces"*, you will undoubtedly run into various challenges.

Remember—
Be patient, mastering melon carving takes practice!

Taking the time to make sure you select suitable melons for carving is the ideal point to start exercising the patience you will require to produce good presentations. If your first selection of fruit does not quite make the grade, take the time now to find a supplier that can provide one that does. Investing a few extra minutes here will insure that the time you will spend carving when you get home will produce the best results.

"When choosing your melons, look for clean, unblemished and large size. By taking the time to hand pick the best melons, you will insure a top quality carving."

Stencil Usage

Grid Enlargement and Reduction Section

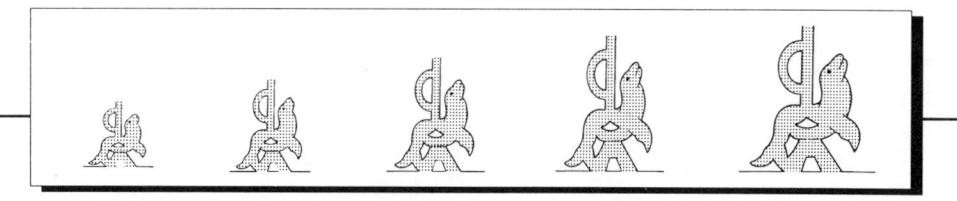

These sections have valuable information. Make sure you study each section carefully and understand before moving on.

By understanding stencil usage and grid enlargement, you do not have to be an artist to carve, you will learn to be a craftsman.

— Stencil Usage Section —

This section is designed to outline the ideas and techniques that will make using your melon stencils simple and safe.

Making a copy of the stencil you want to use is easy! Simply photocopy the stencil, (better photocopy machines allow you to scale your copy to the size you need), or copy the design using heavy tracing paper.

Trim the copy to a workable size. By cutting slits into the edge of the design, it will be easier to attach to the melon's curved surface.

X-ACTO KNIFE —
This is the tool you use to make fine detailed cuts into the melon using your stencil. Other useful tools are shown on pages 15-16-17.

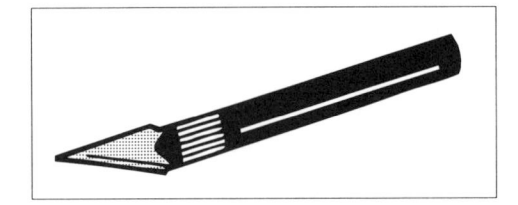

Start by wiping excess moisture off of the melon portion you select for carving (make sure your design is scaled to the right size for the portion you have chosen). Fasten stencil <u>securely</u> to melon using Scotch tape.

Using an X-Acto knife, as shown above, cut a design into the melon using your stencil as a guide, making sure not to cut too deeply at this point. Attach more Scotch tape as needed to keep stencil secure until design is complete. Remove stencil and continue carving, using detailed instructions in stencil section.

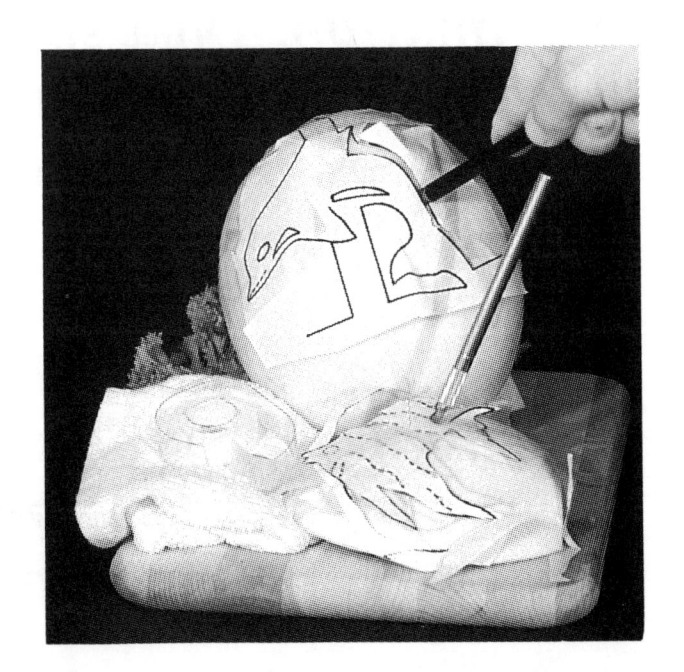

—Grid Enlargement and Reduction—

If you need to enlarge or reduce the designs, the procedure is relatively easy. Using a ruler, draw a square box around the design and divide into even boxes (example shown in 1/4 inches).

Next, using a ruler, draw a square box the size of the design that you would like to enlarge or reduce.

Next, measure the sides and *divide* into the number of *squares* in the *design* that you would like to reduce or enlarge.

Mark box and draw lines to correspond with exact amount of squares, in the smaller or larger design.

Each block should be regarded separately, and the lines of the design that fall in corresponding blocks should be duplicated, (traced) in the stencils new grid.

When finished, you will have an accurately enlarged or reduced pattern design. *(Example is 9 across and 8 up and down)*.

Grid enlargement is very simple, yet complicated. But, by using the grid system you can take a small drawing and enlarge or reduce as needed.

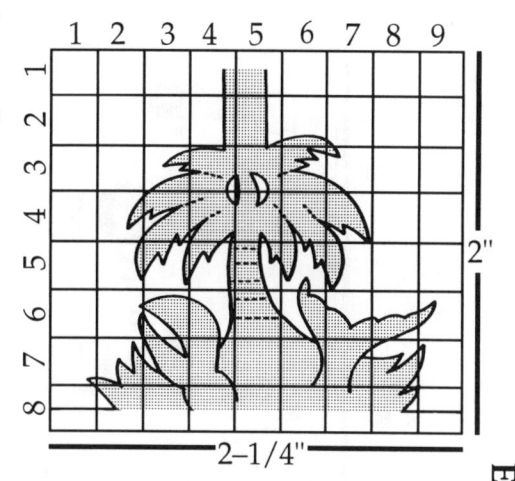

1/4" Inch Squares

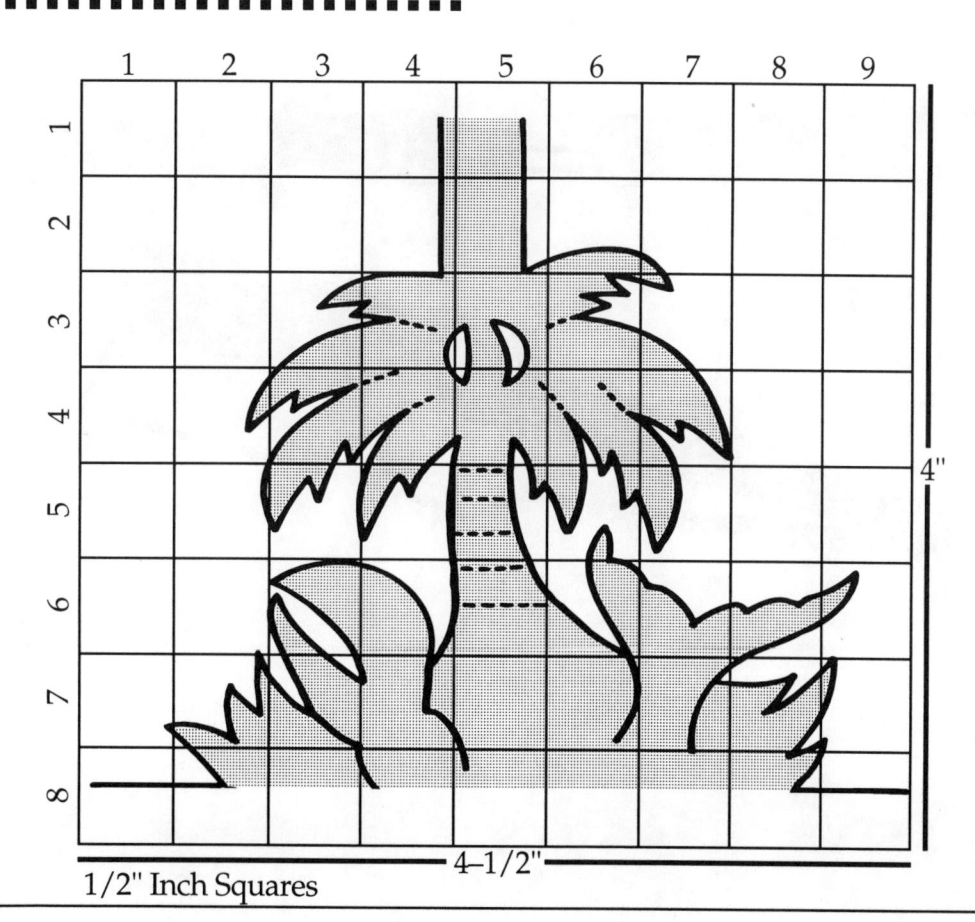

1/2" Inch Squares

EXAMPLES: Shown 1/4 inch to 1/2 inch size enlargement.

13

Tool Usage Section

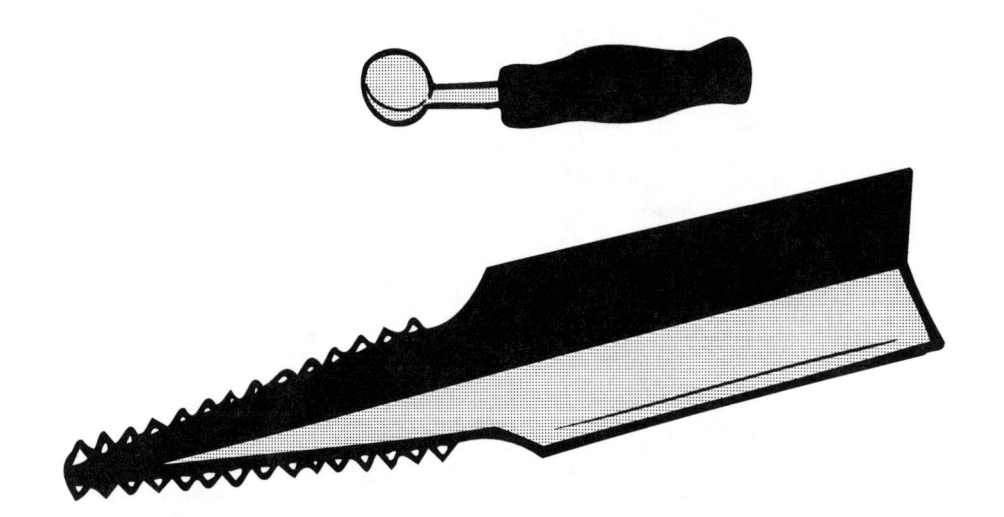

— Tool Usage Section —

PARING KNIFE —
 All purpose knife used for making large and small cuts on fruit.

CHANNEL KNIFE —
 This tool is used for cutting designs in fruit as it removes the outside flesh.

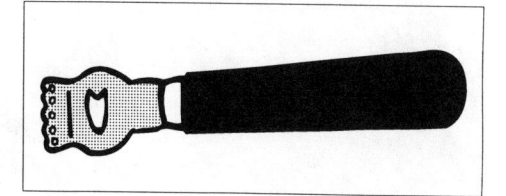

V-TOOL —
 This tool is used to make large and small "V's". (Size of "V's", depends on the depth that the tool is used.)

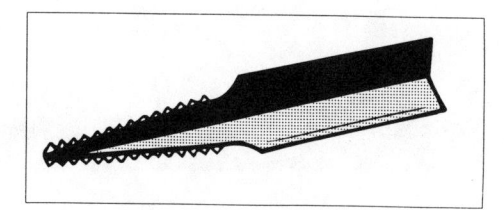

MELON BALLER —
 Used to make melon balls, as well as designs on fruit. Available in plain, fluted and oval styles from $1/8$" to 1".

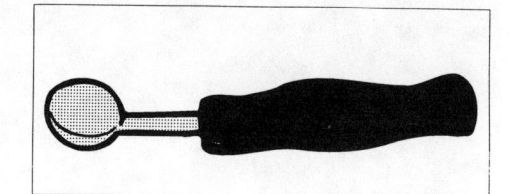

These tools can be purchased at any fine culinary store or from a kitchen supply shop?

— Tool Usage Section —

Paring Knife:
The paring knife is used to make both large and small cuts in your melon design. Keep it sharp and use wrist action to control cuts.

• Paring Knife •

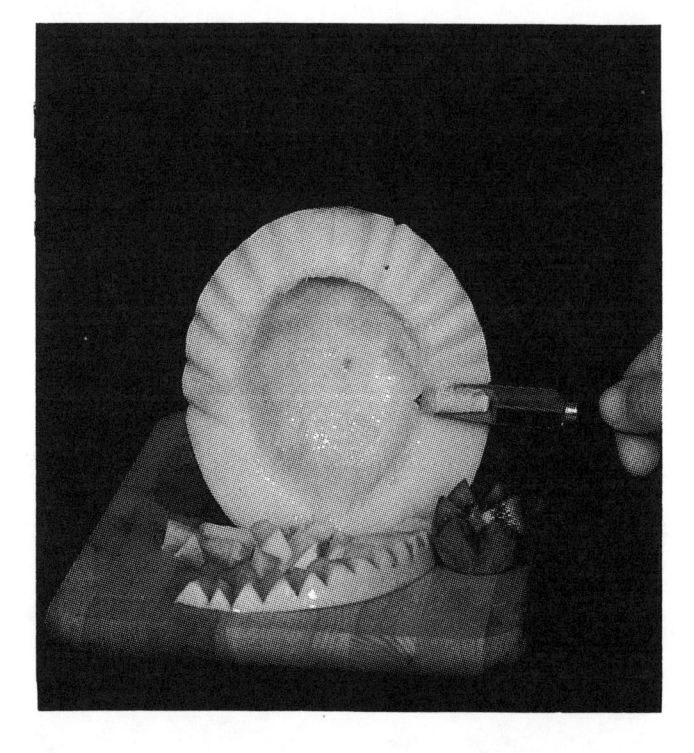

V-Tool:
The V-tool is used to make large or small v-cuts on your melons, depending on how deeply you insert the V-tool. Also, used to make melon crowns & baskets.

• V-Tool •

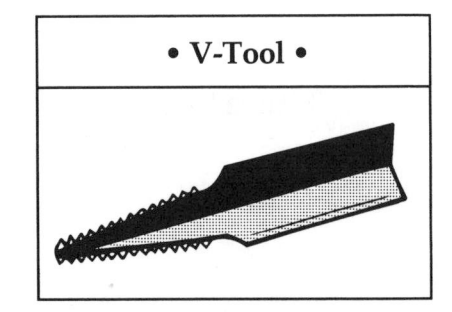

— Tool Usage Section —

Melon Baller:
The melon baller is used to make melon balls, as well as to make various designs on the surface of the melons.

• Melon Baller •

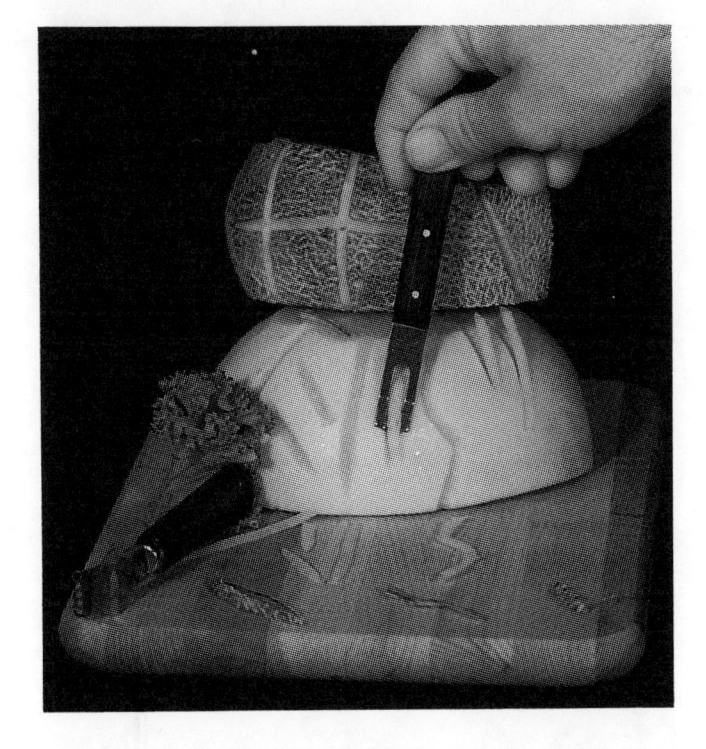

Channel Knife:
The channel knife is used to make surface designs on melons. When using a channel knife be sure to press down hard so the cuts are neat and go deep.

• Channel Knife •

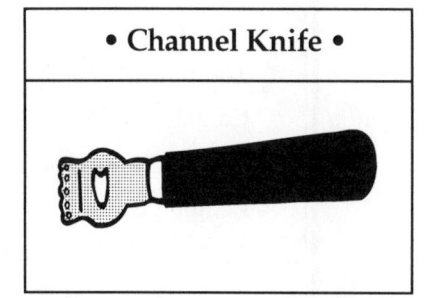

— Decorating Usage Section —

This decorating usage section will give you hints and ideas as to what final touches your melon centerpiece carving will need.

Decorating melon centerpieces can make a great difference in your presentation. By using the background and support materials listed below you can create a wonderful looking melon centerpiece.

Melon centerpieces can be presented in many different ways. They can be on a plate or mirror, with sliced fruit positioned in front of them.

Whether using ferns and flowers, or pineapple tops and purple kale, you can create a centerpiece that can be presented with pride.

Presentations can serve as anchors at each end of buffet tables, or as centerpieces; to set the theme for your special party. They can be supported by glass racks or milk crates covered with table cloths, or glass mirror stands.

As you create and decorate your centerpieces, your creative talents will undoubtedly flow through to your entire presentation as well!

The following is a list of common items that I use to decorate my melon centerpieces. Don't be afraid to experiment with items of your own.

Support and Background Materials

Purple & White Kale	Gold Sword Picks
Melon Balls	Lemon or Lime Crowns
Radish Flowers	Star Fruit
Fresh Fruit, Sliced	Kiwi Fruit
Fresh Berries	Ferns
Flowers (both fresh and dried)	Pineapples (and the tops)
Mint Leaves	Leaf Lettuce
Radicchio	Oranges (cut into crowns)
Toothpicks (wooden)	Toothpick Frills (wooden)
Cantaloupe (cut into crowns)	Honeydew Melon Crowns
Whole Cloves (used as eyes)	Fresh Strawberries
Lemon Leaves	Maraschino Cherries

…and anything else you can think of!

— Hints & Tips —

Repairs and Alterations —

As you, the artist, start to practice *"Mastering the Art of Carving Melon Centerpieces"*, you will undoubtedly run into various challenges. *"Be patient; help is at hand."*

This section on repairs and modifications will give you ideas and techniques on repairing flaws that are bound to occur in the course of each project.

"PATIENCE AND PRACTICE ARE THE TWO INDISPENSABLE VIRTUES IN LEARNING, AND MASTERING, THIS CRAFT."

• Wooden toothpicks and skewers can be used to re-align pieces of melon carvings that fall off.

• Flowers, ferns and (FRESH) fruit, can be used to cover up minor flaws if need be.

• By using imagination and careful, gentle work habits, you can repair just about anything, no matter how major.

"Good luck and be careful."

• **Honeydew Vase**
with Cantaloupe Flower • Pages 54-55 •

• **Christmas Dove Ornament** •
• Pages 34-35 •

— Photo Section —

Cantaloupe Turtle

• **Pages 32-33** •

A cantaloupe carving using cucumber for a head and a carrot for the feet.

A wonderful carving that is easy to make and will bring enjoyment for all to see.

Melon Vase Carving

• **Pages 58-59** •

When carving melon vase carvings, etch design on side of melon. Remove outer melon skin around design. While removing outer skin around design, only go just below the outer skin layer being careful not to go too deep.

After you have mastered this technique, almost all of the stencils in this book will work in carving melon vase carvings.

— Photo Section —

Anchor and Wreath

• Pages 26-27 •

<u>Honeydew carvings with a V-arch background:</u>
Classic Swan • Pages 40-41 •
Honeydew Heart • Pages 52-53 •
Honeydew Vase • Pages 54-55 •
St.Patrick's Pot O' Gold
           • Pages 68-69 •
Honeydew Saint • Pages 84-85 •
Vase • Pages 86-87 •

Quarter Moon

• Pages 64-65 •

<u>Honeydew carvings with a partial V-arch background. The carving is attached at top or sides:</u>
Christmas Dove • Pages 34-35 •
Christmas Reindeer • Pages 36-37 •
Christmas Tree • Pages 38-39 •
Dolphin • Pages 42-43 •
Dove • Pages 46-47 •
Eagle • Pages 48-49 •
Fourth of July Liberty Bell
           • Pages 50-51 •
I Love You • Pages 56-57 •
Palm Tree • Pages 60-61 •
Quarter Moon • Pages 64-65 •
Sailfish • Pages 66-67 •
Seal with Ball • Pages 74-75 •
Southwestern Cactus • Pages 76-77 •
Southwestern Coyote • Pages 78-79 •
Star of David • Pages 80-81 •

— Photo Section —

Dolphins, Three Jumping

• Pages 44-45 •

Similar style carvings to Dolphins:
Banners • Pages 82-83 •
Cantaloupe Flower • Pages 54-55 •
Kissing Doves • Pages 52-53 •
Leaves • Pages 50-51 •
Scallop Shells • Pages 70-71 •
Seaweed • Pages 28-29 & 72-73 •
Swordfish • Pages 82-83 •

These designs are carved on the inside flesh of cantaloupe melons (example shown is Dolphins).

Honeydew Vase with Cantaloupe Flower

• Pages 54-55 •

Similar style carvings:
Honeydew Kissing Doves
• Pages 52-53 •

These designs are partial V-Arch honeydew carvings with cantaloupe carving or carvings toothpicked into place.

By using a combination of carvings you can create a unique effect as shown above and to the left.

— Photo Section —

Seahorse with Seaweed

• Pages 72-73 •

Similar style carving:
Angelfish with Seaweed • Pages 28-29 •
Dolphin, Three Jumping • Pages 44-45 •
Scallop Shell and Palm Tree
                     • Pages 70-71 •
Swordfish with Banners • Pages 82-83 •

These designs use a separate base then the V-arch carvings. Individual carvings are then toothpicked into place.
By using a channel knife you can create a unique affect on the base as shown to the left.

Paradise Fish

• Pages 62-63 •

Relief cuts:
Relief cuts are light precision detailing designs, on melon skin or flesh, removing only the top layer of skin, 1/16 inch deep.
Make relief cuts where broken line is shown.

Carvings with detail cuts:
Angelfish; Bird of Paradise; Christmas Tree; Classic Swan; Dolphins; Eagle; Kissing Doves; Cantaloupe Flower; Palm Tree; Quarter Moon; Paradise Fish; Sailfish; Pot O' Gold; Scallop Shell and Palm Tree; Seahorse; Seal, Cactus; Coyote; Swordfish; Tropical Bird; Honeydew Dragon; and Swan I and II.

— Photo Section —

St. Patrick's Shamrock and Pot O' Gold

• Pages 68-69 •

Multi-piece stencil carvings, using two honeydews.

Similar style carvings:

Paradise Fish	• Pages 62-63 •
Tropical Bird	• Pages 84-85 •
Swan I	• Pages 92-93-94 •
Swan II	• Pages 95-96-97 •

Swan II

• Pages 95-96-97 •

The Swan II is a four-piece stencil carving, using two honeydews.

Similar style carving:
Swan I • Pages 92-93-94 •

Pattern

Culinary Art

Boca Raton, Florida

Stencil Section

Anchor and Wreath

— Melon Required: Honeydew —

— *For detailed tool usage instructions, see pages 12-15-16-17.* —

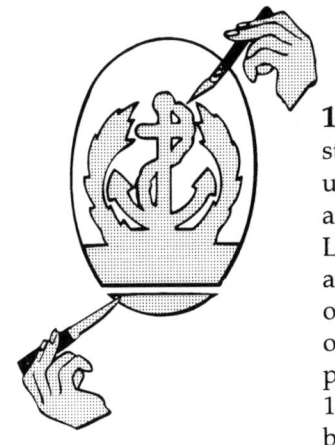

1. Prepare melon and stencil for carving using pattern, tape and X-acto knife. Lightly cut anchor and wreath designs on melon as described on page 12. Be sure to position pattern about 1-1/2" to 2" off the bottom of melon. Cut base as shown.

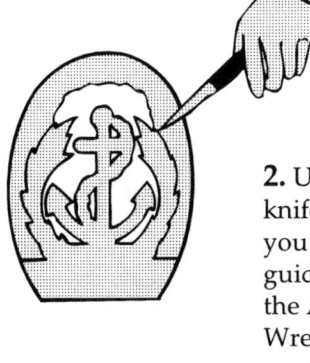

2. Using a paring knife and the pattern you have traced as a guide, start to define the Anchor and Wreath itself, being careful not to carve too deeply into the melon. Refer to illustration on page 21.

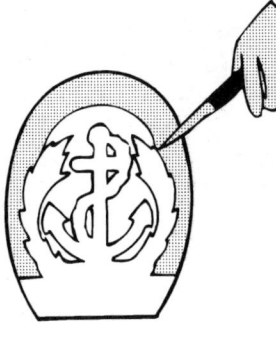

3. After you are satisfied with your carving, work your way toward the back of the melon until the background arch is flat, (which should be halfway toward the rear of the melon).

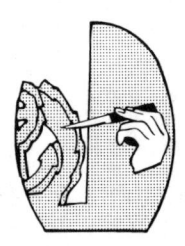

• Side View •

↖ Base

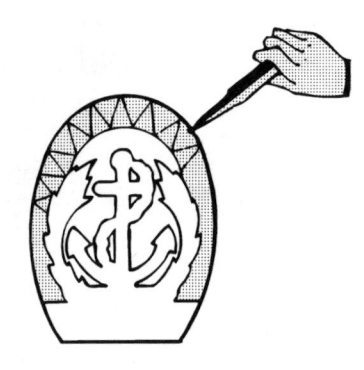

4. Using the V-tool shown above, cut grooves in the background arch to finish your carving. Using a spoon, clean out the inside of the melon.

— *See finishing and decorating ideas on page 18.* —

26

Anchor and Wreath

— For detailed instructions on use of this stencil see pages 11-12. —

— *See illustration on page 21 for reference.* —

Angelfish with Seaweed

— Melons Required: Honeydew and Cantaloupe —

— *For detailed tool usage instructions, see pages 12-15-16-17.* —

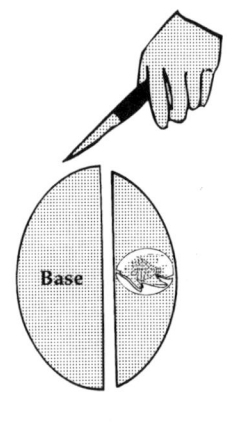

1. Using the honeydew melon cut lengthwise into two sections, one roughly three times the size of the other as shown. Remember you will be carving the Angelfish out of the small piece and using the large piece for a base.

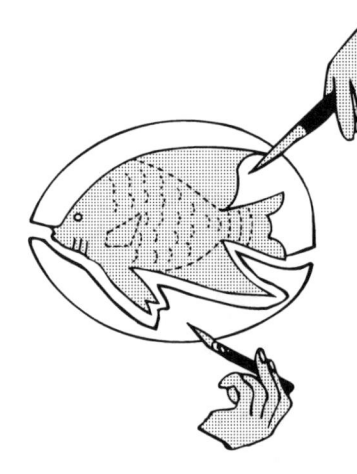

2. Prepare small melon section and Angelfish stencil for carving using pattern, tape and X-acto knife. Lightly cut Angelfish design on melon as described on page 12. Using a paring knife and the pattern you have traced as a guide, start to define the Angelfish itself. Add detail on broken lines as needed. Refer to photo section on page 23.

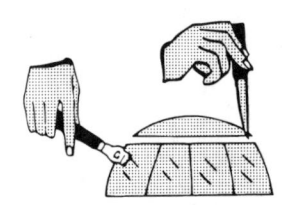

3. Cut off a small section of the base piece of the honeydew, using a paring knife. This will act as a base.

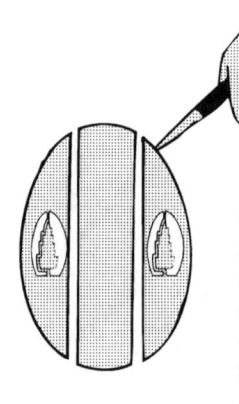

4. Using the cantaloupe melon cut lengthwise into three sections, as shown. Remember you will be carving the Seaweed out of each side piece.

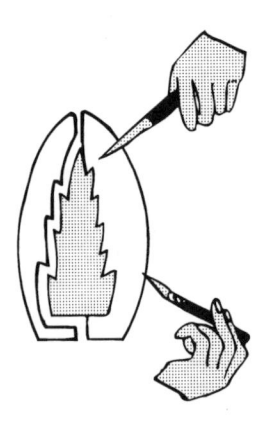

5. Prepare the two melon sections and Seaweed stencil for carving using pattern, tape and X-acto knife. Lightly cut Seaweed on inside skin of melon sections. Using a paring knife and the patterns you have traced as a guide, define the Seaweed themselves. Refer to photo section on page 22.

6. Assemble carving with toothpicks, referring to photo sections.

— *See finishing and decorating ideas on page 18.* —

Angelfish with Seaweed

— For detailed instructions on use of this stencil see pages 11-12. —

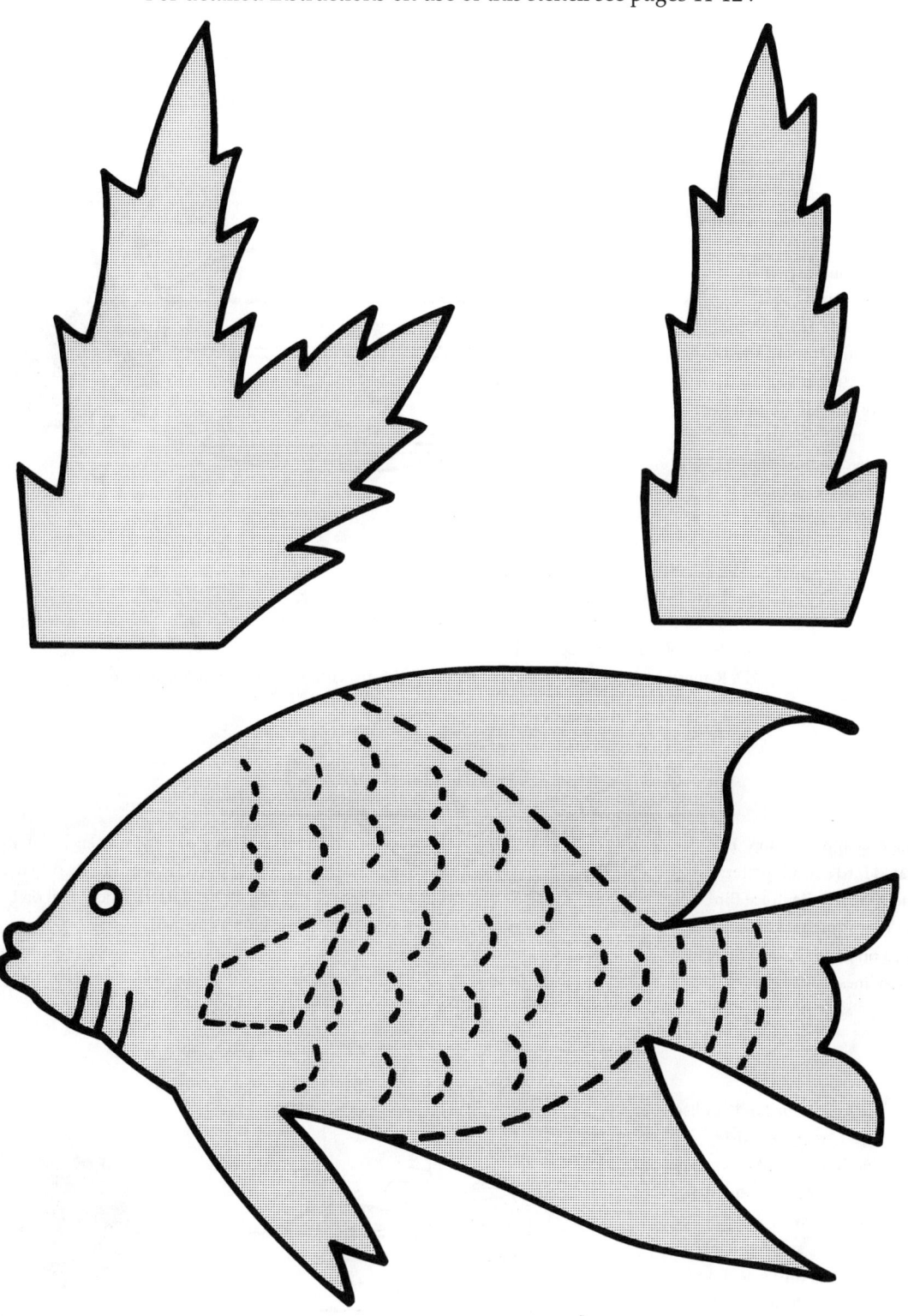

— See illustration on page 23 for reference. —

—NOTE—
Broken lines are shown to indicate relief and detail only, and should never be cut through!

Bird of Paradise

— Pineapple and Apple or Orange Required —

— For detailed tool usage instructions, see pages 12-15-16-17. —

1. Section the pineapple using a paring knife, (slicer or french knife) as in the illustration A to D. When cutting section C (body), be careful to leave the pineapple's leafy top attached to this section. (Leafy top will be birds feather's and tail.)

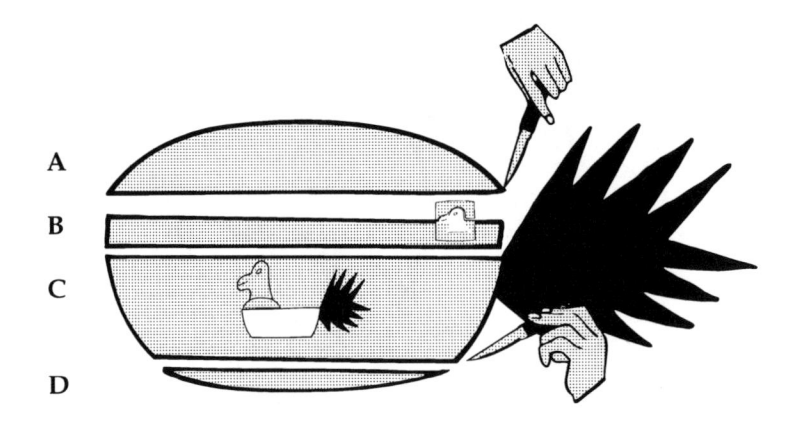

A
B
C
D

SECTION BREAKDOWN:
A. Extra piece (first cut). Not needed for design.
B. To be used for bird's head. Cut about 1/2-3/4 inch thick (second cut).
C. Body of Bird of Paradise (third cut).
D. Remove to form base on Bird of Paradise (fourth cut). Last piece not needed.

2. Using pineapple section "B" designated bird's head, pattern, tape and X-acto knife, trace Bird's head on pineapple section as described on page 12. Add detail on broken lines.

3. Using paring knife and the pattern you have traced as a guide, start to define the Bird's head itself. Add detail on broken lines as needed.

4. Attach Bird of Paradise head, as shown, using toothpicks. Cut an apple or orange into four quarters. Attach one of these quarters, positioning between Bird's neck and body, with toothpicks.

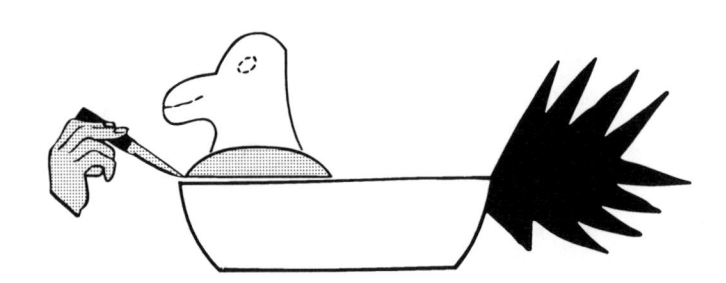

— See finishing and decorating ideas on page 18. —

30

Bird of Paradise

— For detailed instructions on use of this stencil see pages 11-12. —

• Hat Pattern •

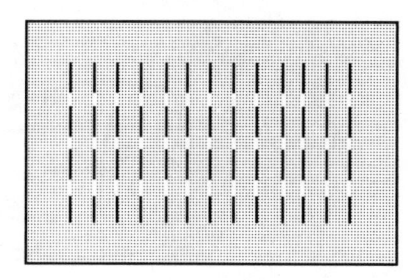

• Hat Pattern folded in 1/2 •

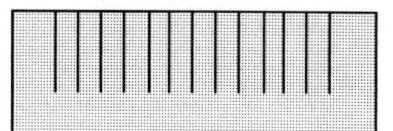

5. To make the Bird of Paradise hat, cut a piece of tin foil about 4" by 2 1/2" inches. Cut lines as shown, using a X-acto knife. Fold hat in half, adjust hat around pineapple head, tape ends together. Next toothpick in place on Bird of Paradise head.

— NOTE —
Broken lines are shown to indicate relief and detail only, and should never be cut through!

Cantaloupe Turtle

— Melon Required: Cantaloupe, Cucumber and Carrot —

— For detailed tool usage instructions, see pages 12-15-16-17. —

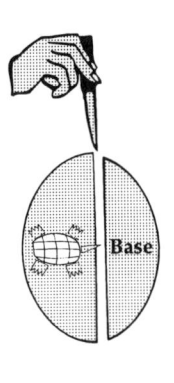

1. To start this carving cut cantaloupe melon lengthwise into two sections, one roughly three times the size of the other as shown. Remember you will be carving the turtle's body out of the large piece and using the small piece for the base.

2. Using a paring knife cut off one end of cantaloupe, (large piece) as shown. Be careful not to carve too deep into melon as this is where the cucumber head will be attached. Next, using a channel knife make grooves in cantaloupe as shown. Design should resemble a turtle body when done. Refer to illustration on page 20.

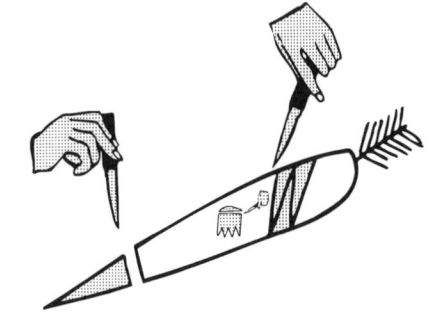

3. Using toothpicks assemble base with body as shown.

4. Using a paring knife cut four large V's out of a large peeled carrot. V's are to be used for feet of turtle. Next, cut off end of carrot (2-2 1/2 inches long). Cut in half to form tail for turtle as shown.

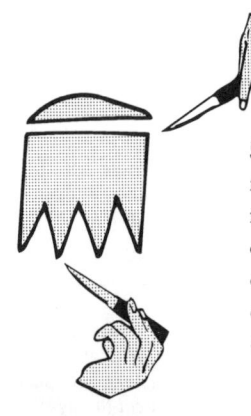

5. Using a paring knife and the four carrot V's, cut three small V's in the thin end, to form toes on carrots. Cut off small section of carrot on thick end, (this is where carrot will be attached to cantaloupe in next step).

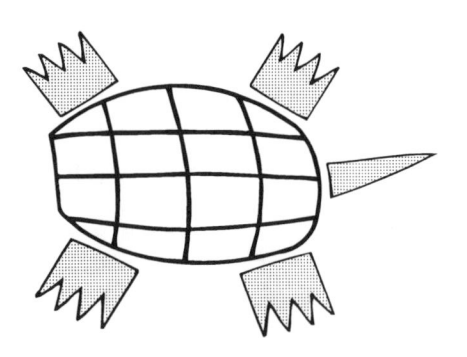

6. Using toothpicks attach feet and tail on turtle as shown. Refer to illustration on page 20. (Remember flat end of cantaloupe is for turtle head not the tail).

— See finishing and decorating ideas on page 18. —

Cantaloupe Turtle

— For detailed instructions on use of this stencil see pages 11-12. —

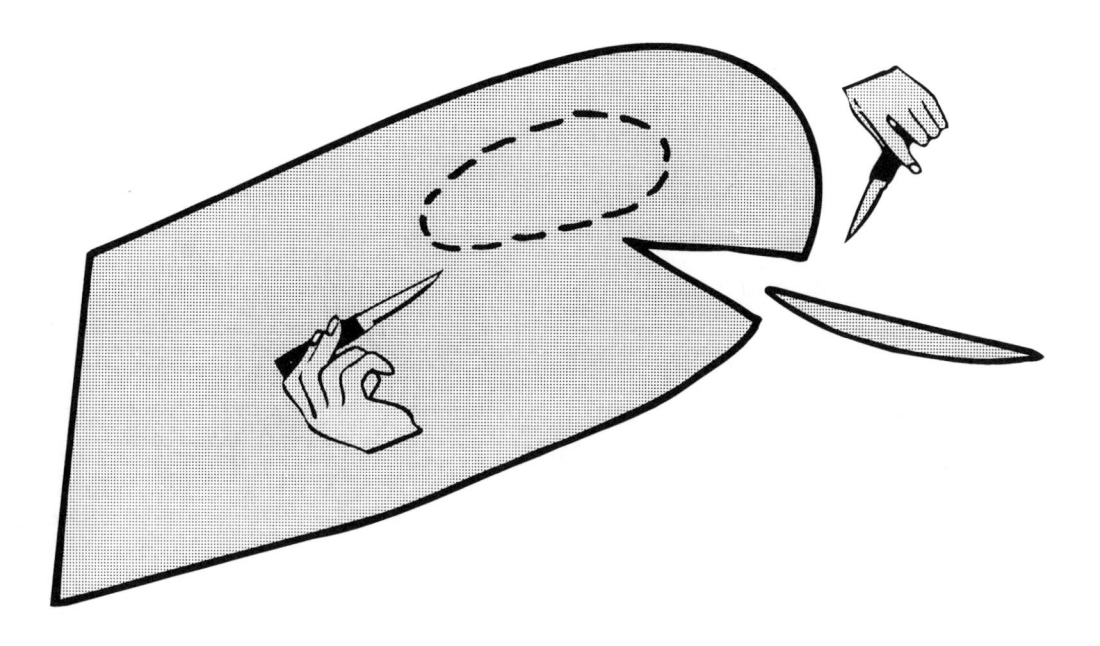

7. Using a paring knife and a cucumber or zucchini cut turtle head as shown, (cut at an angle for turtle head to rise up). For the eyes, cut off medium size patch on both sides of head (shave off skin only). By using small slice of black olive or red grape you can form eye of turtle. Next, cut out section for mouth, by using a slice of red pepper or carrot you can form a tongue, cut small hole inside mouth and place end of tongue inside until secure.

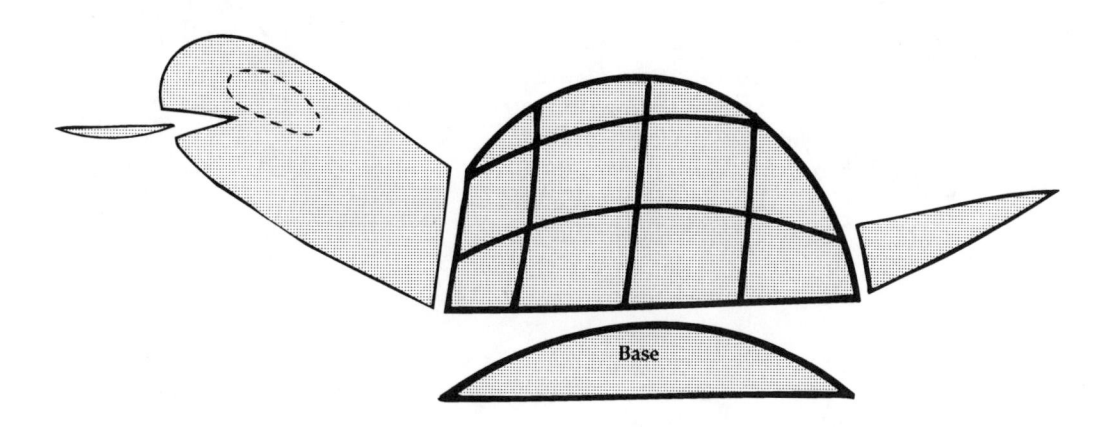

8. Using toothpicks assemble cucumber head on turtle base as shown (use a lot of toothpicks to hold in place).

— *See illustration on page 20 for reference.* —

Christmas Dove Ornament

— Melon Required: Honeydew —

— *For detailed tool usage instructions, see pages 12-15-16-17.* —

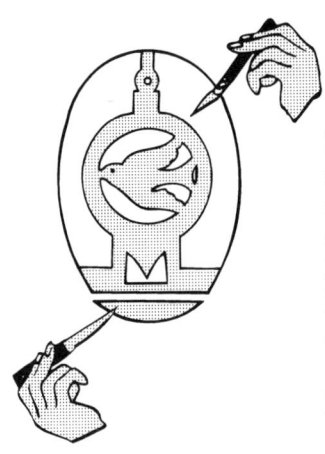

1. Prepare melon and stencil for carving using pattern, tape and X-acto knife. Lightly cut Christmas Dove design on melon as described on page 12. Be sure to position pattern about 1-1/2" to 2" off the bottom of melon. Cut base as shown.

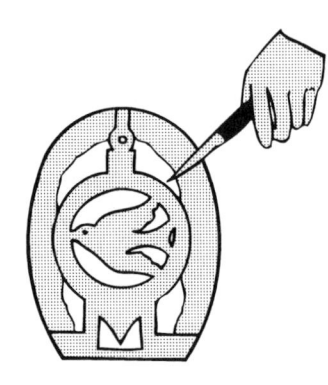

2. Using a paring knife and the pattern you have traced as a guide, start to define the Christmas Dove itself, being careful not to detach top, or carve too deeply into the melon. Refer to illustration on pages 19 and 21.

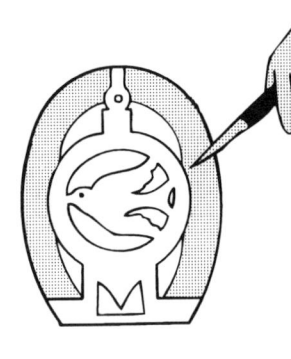

• Side View •

↖ Base

3. After you are satisfied with your carving, work your way toward the back of the melon until the background arch is flat, (which should be halfway toward the rear of the melon). Do not detach top of carving from melon.

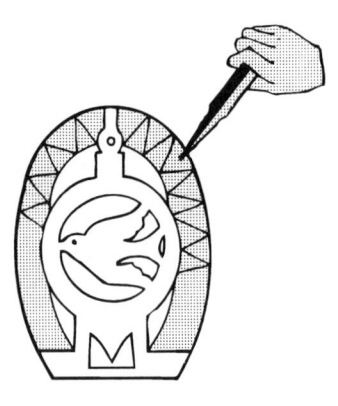

4. Using the V-tool shown above, cut grooves in the background arch to finish your carving. Using a spoon, clean out the inside of the melon.

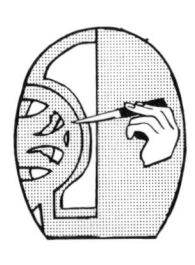

— *See finishing and decorating ideas on page 18.* —

Christmas Dove Ornament

— For detailed instructions on use of this stencil see pages 11-12. —

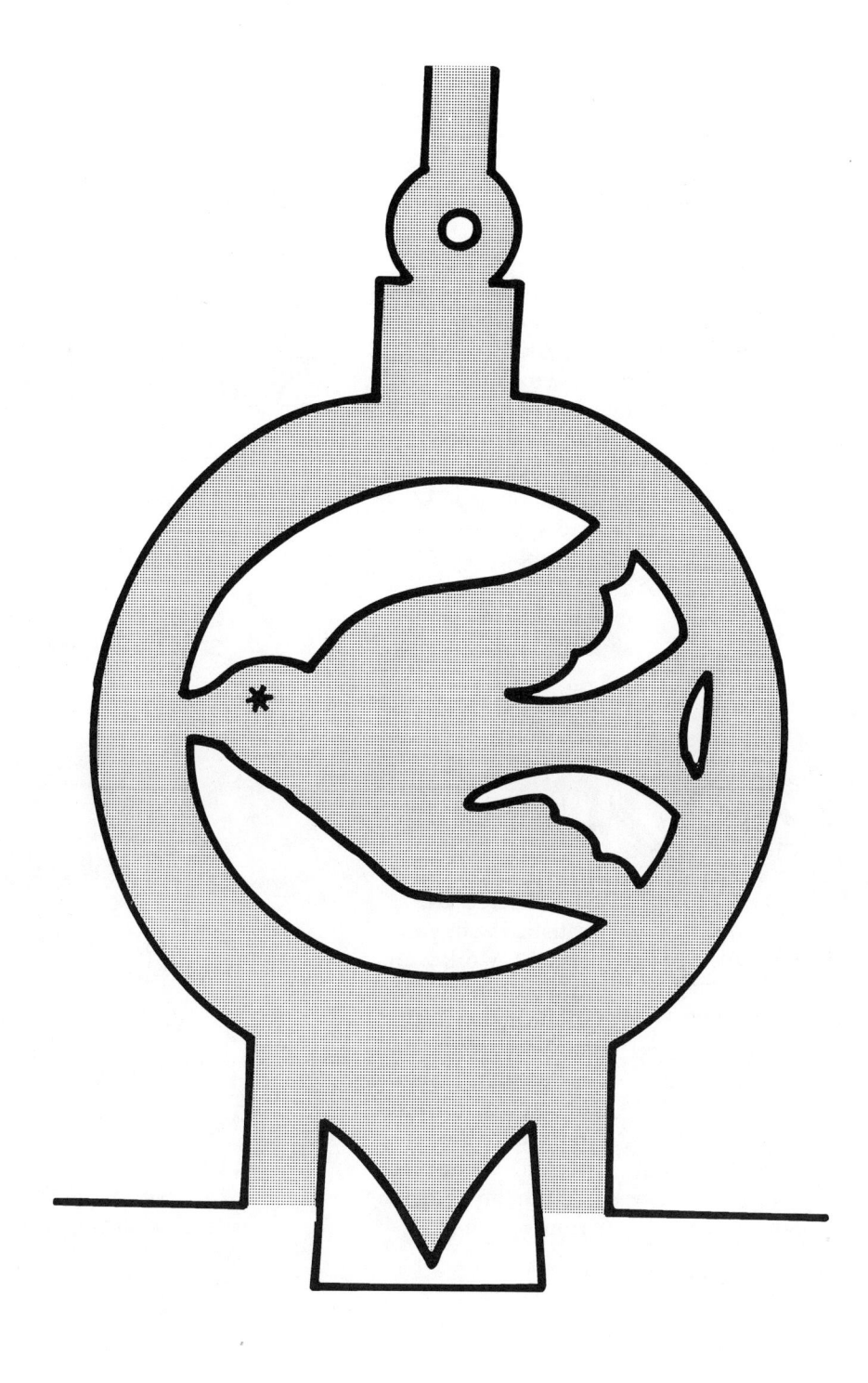

— *See illustration on pages 19 and 21 for reference.* —

Christmas Reindeer

— Melon Required: Honeydew —

— *For detailed tool usage instructions, see pages 12-15-16-17.* —

1. Prepare melon and stencil for carving using pattern, tape and X-acto knife. Lightly cut Christmas Reindeer design on melon as described on page 12. Be sure to position pattern about 1-1/2" to 2" off the bottom of melon. Cut base as shown.

2. Using a paring knife and the pattern you have traced as a guide, start to define the Christmas Reindeer itself, being careful not to detach top, or carve too deeply into the melon. Refer to illustration on page 21.

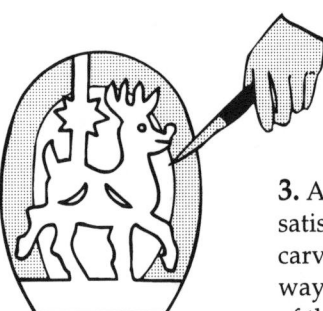

3. After you are satisfied with your carving, work your way toward the back of the melon until the background arch is flat, (which should be halfway toward the rear of the melon). Do not detach top of carving from melon.

• Side View •

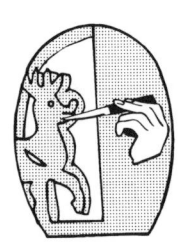

↖ Base

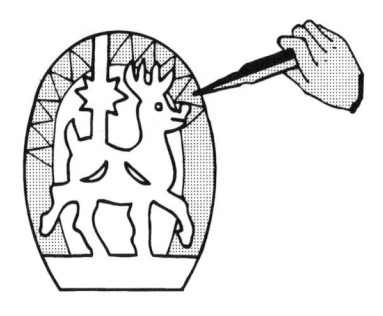

4. Using the V-tool shown above, cut grooves in the background arch to finish your carving. Using a spoon, clean out the inside of the melon.

— *See finishing and decorating ideas on page 18.* —

36

Christmas Reindeer

— For detailed instructions on use of this stencil see pages 11-12. —

— *See illustration on page 21 for reference.* —

Christmas Tree

— Melon Required: Honeydew —

— *For detailed tool usage instructions, see pages 12-15-16-17.* —

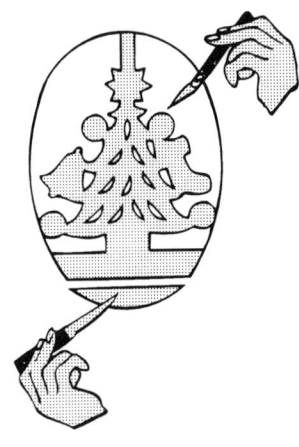

1. Prepare melon and stencil for carving using pattern, tape and X-acto knife. Lightly cut Christmas Tree design on melon as described on page 12. Be sure to position pattern about 1-1/2" to 2" off the bottom of melon. Cut base as shown.

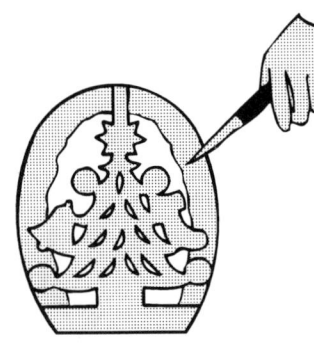

2. Using a paring knife and the pattern you have traced as a guide, start to define the Christmas Tree itself, being careful not to detach top, or carve too deeply into the melon. Refer to illustration on page 21.

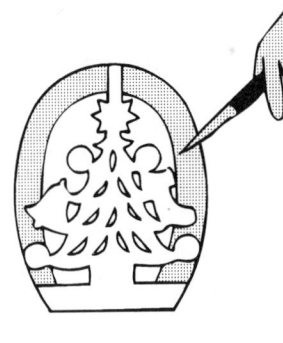

• Side View •

↖ Base

3. After you are satisfied with your carving, work your way toward the back of the melon until the background arch is flat, (which should be halfway toward the rear of the melon). Do not detach top of carving from melon.

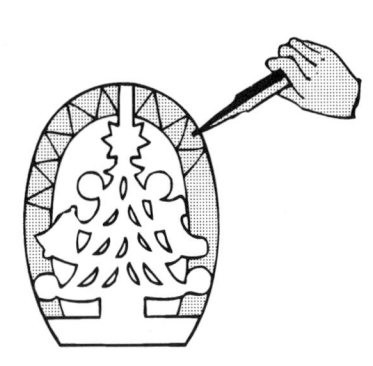

4. Using the V-tool shown above, cut grooves in the background arch to finish your carving. Using a spoon, clean out the inside of the melon.

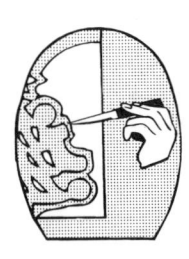

— *See finishing and decorating ideas on page 18.* —

Christmas Tree

— For detailed instructions on use of this stencil see pages 11-12. —

— *See illustration on page 21 for reference.* —

Classic Swan

— Melon Required: Honeydew —

— For detailed tool usage instructions, see pages 12-15-16-17. —

1. Prepare melon and stencil for carving using pattern, tape and X-acto knife. Lightly cut Classic Swan design on melon as described on page 12. Be sure to position pattern about 1-1/2" to 2" off the bottom of melon. Cut base as shown.

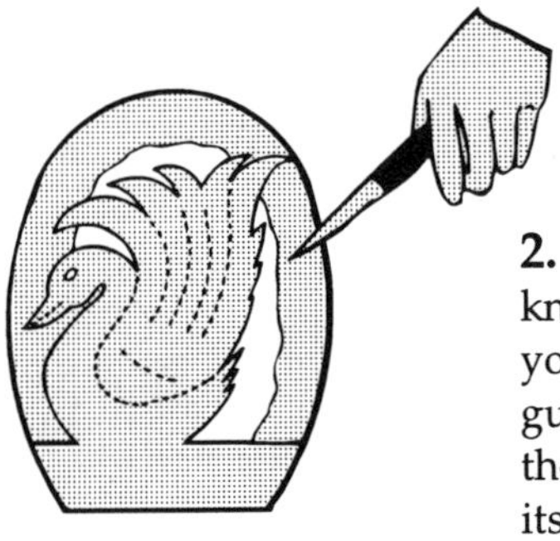

2. Using a paring knife and the pattern you have traced as a guide, start to define the Classic Swan itself, being careful not to carve too deeply into the melon. Add detail on broken lines as needed. Refer to illustration on page 21.

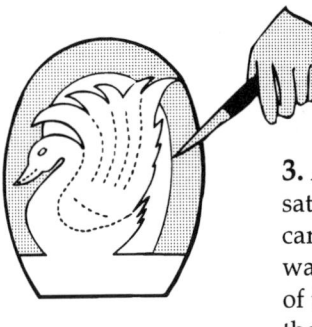

• Side View •

3. After you are satisfied with your carving, work your way toward the back of the melon until the background arch is flat, (which should be halfway toward the rear of the melon). Do not detach top of carving from melon.

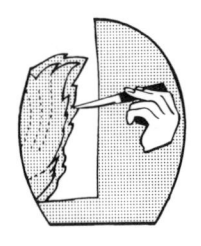

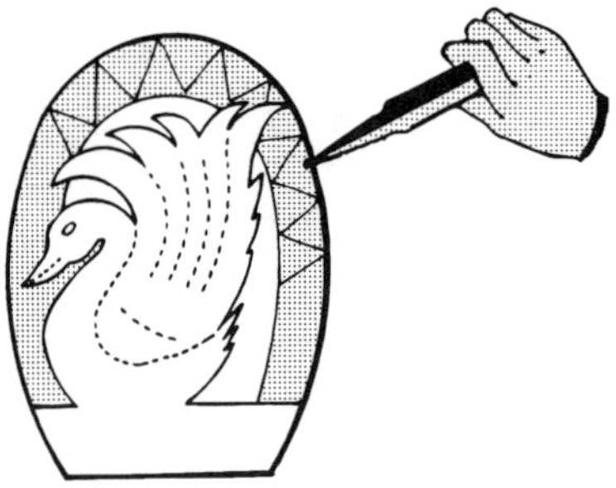

4. Using the V-tool shown above, cut grooves in the background arch to finish your carving. Using a spoon, clean out the inside of the melon.

— See finishing and decorating ideas on page 18. —

Classic Swan

— For detailed instructions on use of this stencil see pages 11-12. —

— See illustration on page 21 for reference. —

> **— NOTE —**
> Broken lines are shown to indicate relief and detail only, and should never be cut through!

Dolphin

— Melon Required: Honeydew —

— *For detailed tool usage instructions, see pages 12-15-16-17.* —

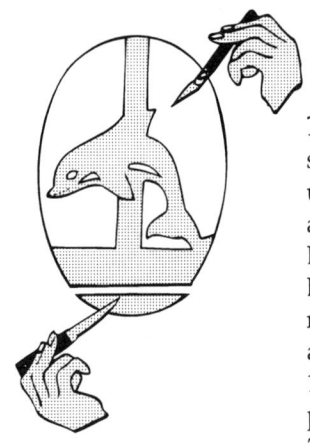

1. Prepare melon and stencil for carving using pattern, tape and X-acto knife. Lightly cut Dolphin design on melon as described on page 12. Be sure to position pattern about 1-1/2" to 2" off the bottom of melon. Cut base as shown.

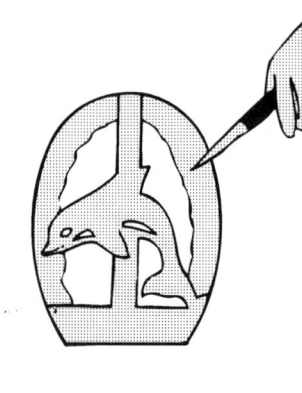

2. Using a paring knife and the pattern you have traced as a guide, start to define the Dolphin itself, being careful not to detach top, or carve too deeply into the melon. Add detail on broken lines as needed. Refer to illustration on page 21.

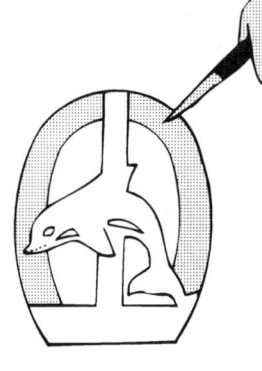

3. After you are satisfied with your carving, work your way toward the back of the melon until the background arch is flat, (which should be halfway toward the rear of the melon). Do not detach top of carving from melon.

• Side View •

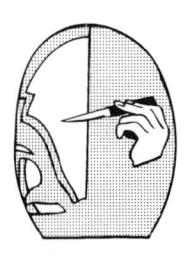

↖ Base

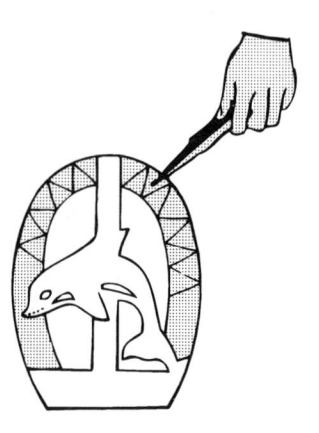

4. Using the V-tool shown above, cut grooves in the background arch to finish your carving. Using a spoon, clean out the inside of the melon.

— *See finishing and decorating ideas on page 18.* —

42

Dolphin

— For detailed instructions on use of this stencil see pages 11-12. —

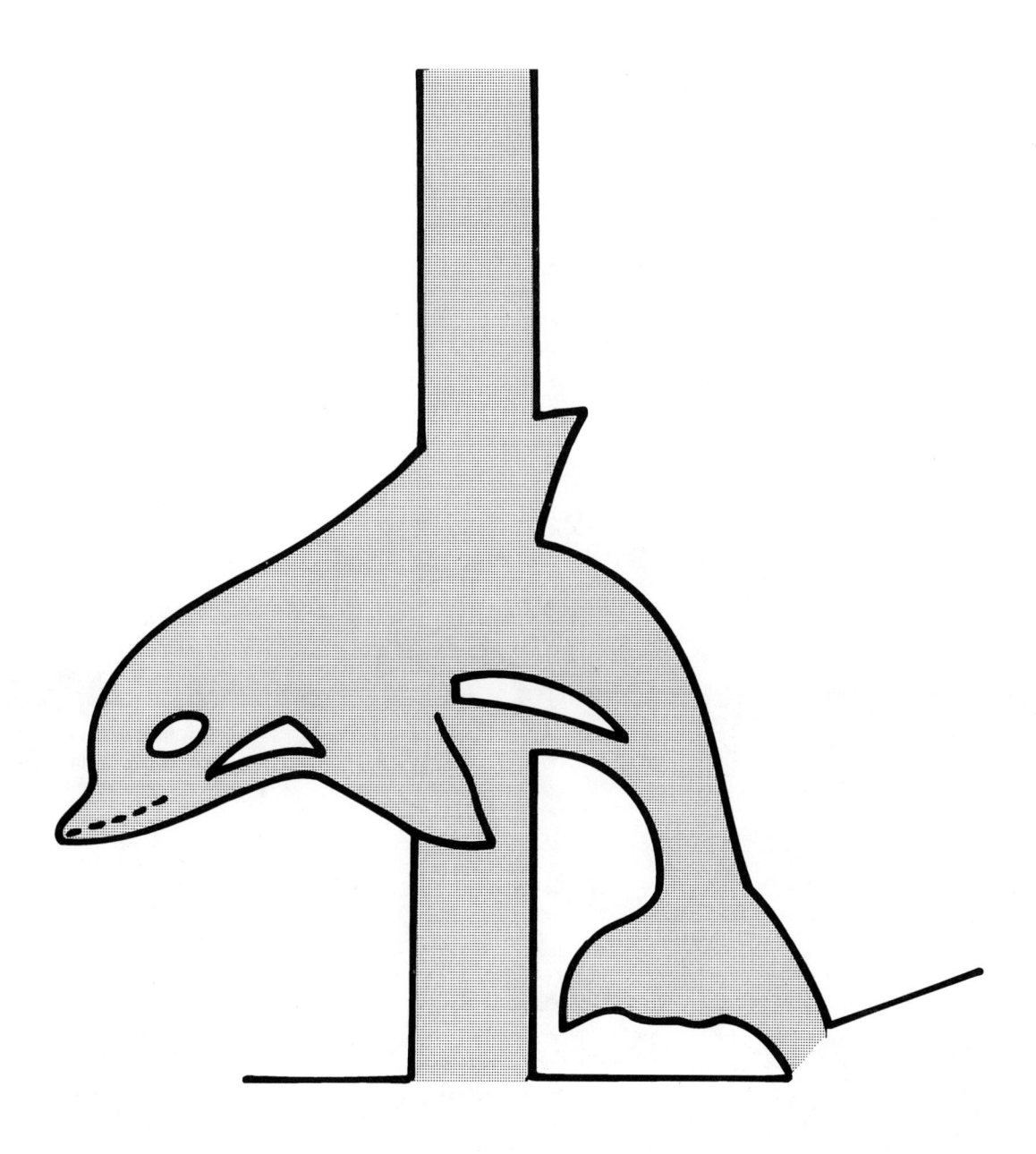

— *See illustration on page 21 for reference.* —

Dolphins, Three Jumping

— Melons Required: Two Cantaloupes —

— *For detailed tool usage instructions, see pages 12-15-16-17.* —

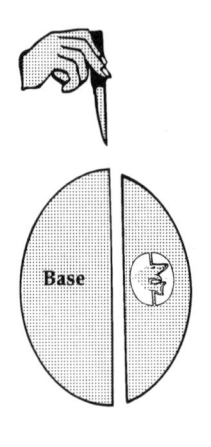

1. To start this carving, first cut one cantaloupe melon lengthwise into two sections one roughly three times the size of the other, as shown. Remember you will be carving one Dolphin out of the smaller piece, with the larger piece acting as a base, so cut accordingly!

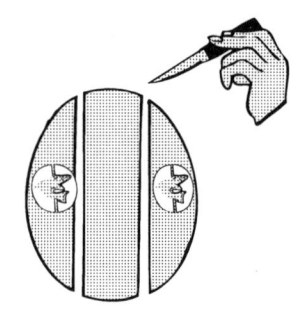

2. Next, take second cantaloupe and cut lengthwise into three sections as shown. Remember you will be carving Dolphins out of each side piece.

3. Using the three sections reserved for Dolphins, prepare melon sections and stencil for carving using patterns, tape and X-acto knife. Lightly cut Dolphins on each melon piece on inside flesh as described on page 12. Refer to illustration on page 22.

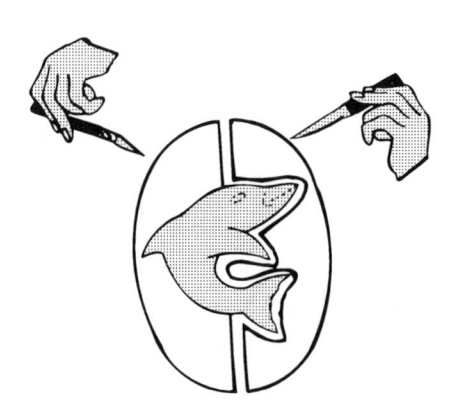

4. Using a paring knife and the patterns you have traced as guides, start to define the Dolphins themselves. Add detail on broken lines as needed. Refer to illustration on page 22.

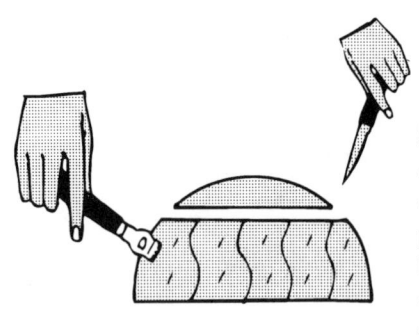

5. Using the large cantaloupe section designated for base remove portion of melon to act as a base, using channel knife and example remove outer skin as indicated to complete base.

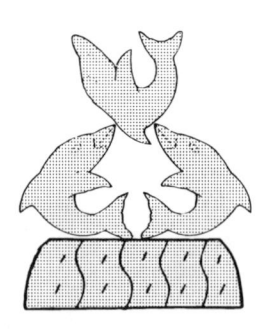

6. Assemble carving with toothpicks, referring to illustration and photo section.

— *See finishing and decorating ideas on page 18.* —

Dolphins, Three Jumping

— For detailed instructions on use of this stencil see pages 11-12. —

— See illustration on page 22 for reference. —

```
— NOTE —
Broken lines are shown to
indicate relief and detail
only, and should never be
cut through!
```

Dove

— Melon Required: Honeydew —

— *For detailed tool usage instructions, see pages 12-15-16-17.* —

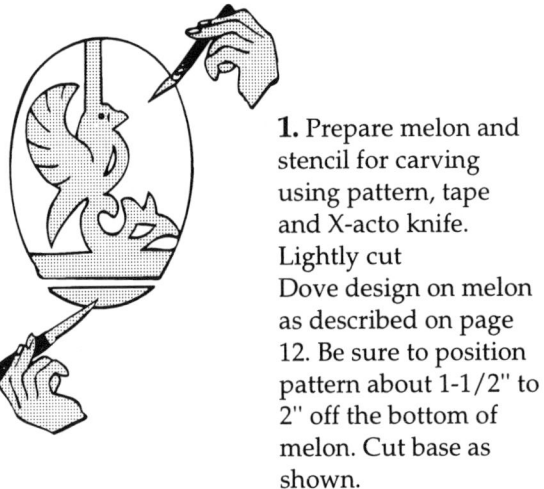

1. Prepare melon and stencil for carving using pattern, tape and X-acto knife. Lightly cut Dove design on melon as described on page 12. Be sure to position pattern about 1-1/2" to 2" off the bottom of melon. Cut base as shown.

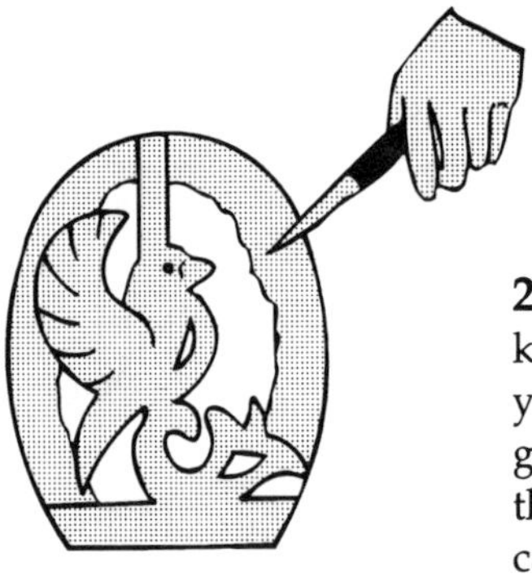

2. Using a paring knife and the pattern you have traced as a guide, start to define the Dove itself, being careful not to detach top, or carve too deeply into the melon. Add detail on broken lines as needed. Refer to illustration on page 21.

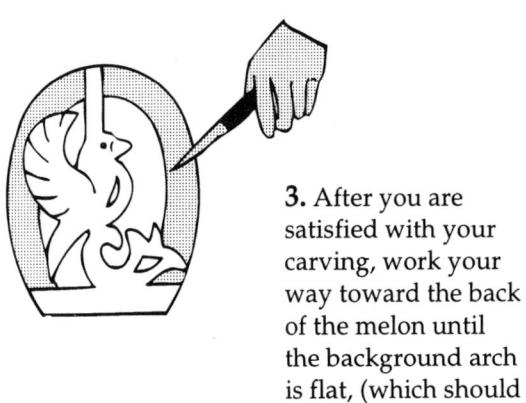

• Side View •

3. After you are satisfied with your carving, work your way toward the back of the melon until the background arch is flat, (which should be halfway toward the rear of the melon). Do not detach top of carving from melon.

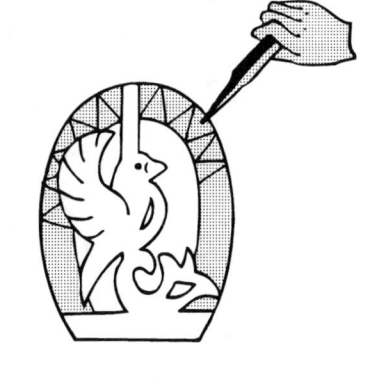

↖ Base

4. Using the V-tool shown above, cut grooves in the background arch to finish your carving. Using a spoon, clean out the inside of the melon.

— *See finishing and decorating ideas on page 18.* —

Dove

— For detailed instructions on use of this stencil see pages 11-12. —

— *See illustration on page 21 for reference.* —

Eagle

— Melon Required: Honeydew —

— *For detailed tool usage instructions, see pages 12-15-16-17.* —

1. Prepare melon and stencil for carving using pattern, tape and X-acto knife. Lightly cut Eagle design on melon as described on page 12. Be sure to position pattern about 1-1/2" to 2" off the bottom of melon. Cut base as shown.

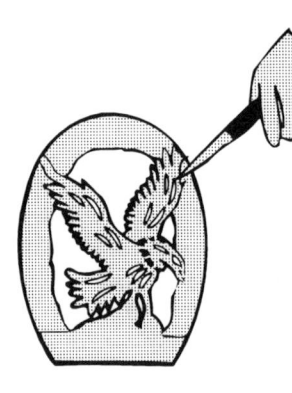

2. Using a paring knife and the pattern you have traced as a guide, start to define the Eagle itself, being careful not to detach tops, or carve too deeply into the melon. Add detail on broken lines as needed. Refer to illustration on page 21.

3. After you are satisfied with your carving, work your way toward the back of the melon until the background arch is flat, (which should be halfway toward the rear of the melon). Do not detach top of carving from melon.

• Side View •

↖ Base

4. Using the V-tool shown above, cut grooves in the background arch to finish your carving. Using a spoon, clean out the inside of the melon.

— *See finishing and decorating ideas on page 18.* —

48

Eagle

— For detailed instructions on use of this stencil see pages 11-12. —

— *See illustration on page 21 for reference.* —

— **NOTE** —
Broken lines are shown to indicate relief and detail only, and should never be cut through!

Fourth of July Liberty Bell

— Melons Required: Honeydew —

— For detailed tool usage instructions, see pages 12-15-16-17. —

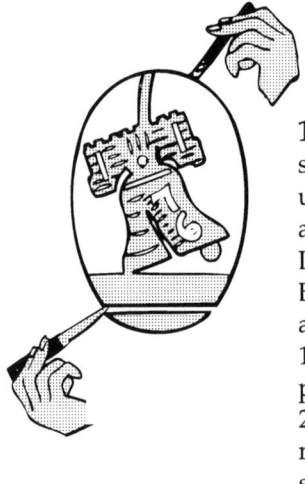

1. Prepare melon and stencil for carving using pattern, tape and X-acto knife. Lightly cut Bell design on melon as described on page 12. Be sure to position pattern about 1-1/2" to 2" off the bottom of melon. Cut base as shown.

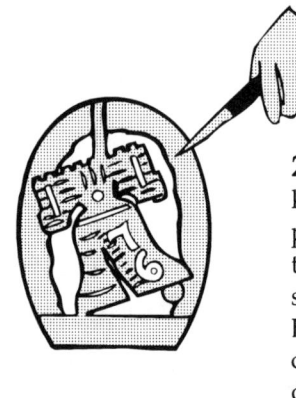

2. Using a paring knife and the pattern you have traced as a guide, start to define the Bell itself, being careful not to detach tops, or carve too deeply into the melon. Add detail on broken lines as needed. Refer to illustration on page 21.

• Side View •

↖ Base

3. After you are satisfied with your carving, work your way toward the back of the melon until the background arch is flat, (which should be halfway toward the rear of the melon). Do not detach top of carving from melon.

4. Using the V-tool shown above, cut grooves in the background arch to finish your carving. Using a spoon, clean out the inside of the melon.

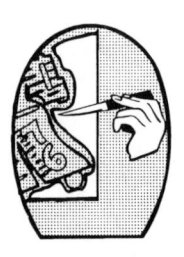

— See finishing and decorating ideas on page 18. —

Fourth of July Liberty Bell

— For detailed instructions on use of this stencil see pages 11-12. —

— *See illustration on page 21 for reference.*—

```
— NOTE —
Broken lines are shown to
indicate relief and detail
only, and should never be
cut through!
```

Honeydew Kissing Doves

— Melons Required: Honeydew and Cantaloupe —

— *For detailed tool usage instructions, see pages 12-15-16-17.* —

1. Prepare honeydew melon and stencil for carving using pattern, tape and X-acto knife. Lightly cut Heart design on melon as described on page 12. Be sure to position pattern about 1-1/2" to 2" off the bottom of melon. Cut base as shown.

2. Using a paring knife and the pattern you have traced as a guide, start to define the Heart itself, being careful not to carve too deeply into the melon. Add detail on broken lines as needed. Refer to illustration on page 21.

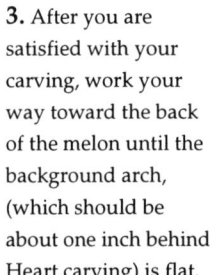

3. After you are satisfied with your carving, work your way toward the back of the melon until the background arch, (which should be about one inch behind Heart carving) is flat.

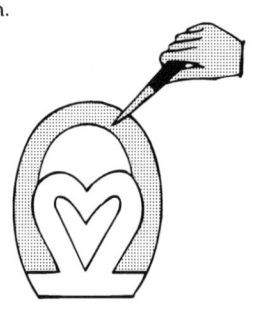

4. Using the V-tool shown above, cut grooves in the background arch to finish your Heart carving. Using a spoon, clean out the inside of the melon.

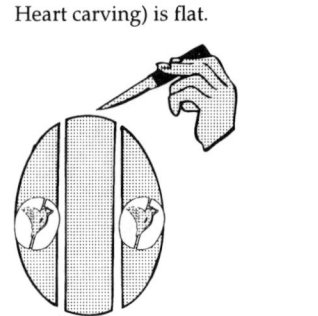

5. Using the 2nd melon, cut cantaloupe lengthwise into three sections as shown. Remember you will be carving the side sections into Doves.

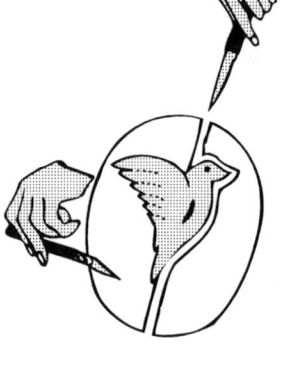

6. Prepare melon sections and stencil for carving using pattern, tape and X-acto knife Lightly cut Doves in each section on skin of melons. Using a paring knife and the patterns you have traced as a guide define the carvings themselves. Refer to illustration on page 22.

7. Assemble carving with toothpicks, referring to illustration on page 22.

— *See finishing and decorating ideas on page 18.* —

52

Honeydew Kissing Doves

— For detailed instructions on use of this stencil see pages 11-12. —

— *See illustration on pages 21-22 for reference.* —

— NOTE —
Broken lines are shown to indicate relief and detail only, and should never be cut through!

Honeydew Vase with Cantaloupe Flower

— Melons Required: Honeydew and Cantaloupe —

— For detailed tool usage instructions, see pages 12-15-16-17. —

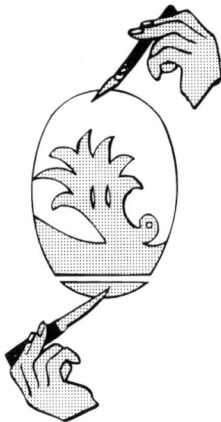

1. Prepare melon and stencil for carving using pattern, tape and X-acto knife. Lightly cut Vase design on honeydew melon as described on page 12. Be sure to position pattern about 1-1/2" to 2" off the bottom of melon. Cut base as shown.

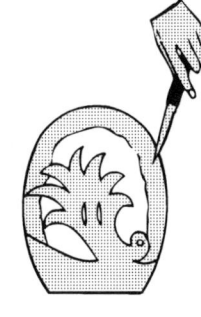

2. Using a paring knife and the pattern you have traced as a guide, start to define the Vase itself, being careful not to carve too deeply into the melon. Add detail on broken lines as needed. Refer to illustration on page 21.

3. After you are satisfied with your carving, work your way toward the back of the melon until the background arch, (which should be halfway toward the rear of the melon) is flat.

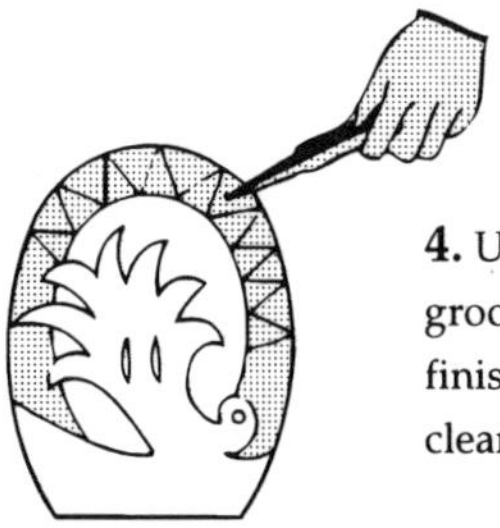

4. Using the V-tool shown, cut grooves in the background arch to finish your carving. Using a spoon, clean out the inside of the melon.

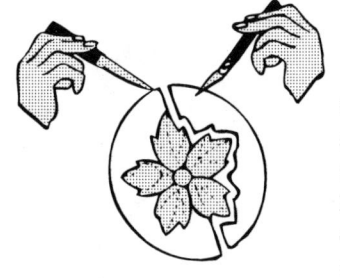

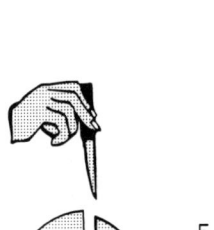

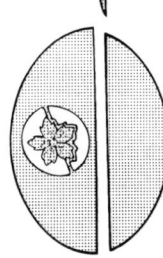

5. Using the cantaloupe melon cut lengthwise into two sections, one roughly three times the size of the other as shown. Remember, you will be carving the Flower out of the large piece and the small piece is extra.

6. Prepare melon section and stencil for carving using pattern, tape and X-acto knife. Lightly cut Flower on inside flesh of cantaloupe melon section. Using the pattern you have traced as a guide, define the carving itself. Add detail on broken lines as needed. Refer to illustration on page 22.

7. Assemble carving with toothpicks, referring to illustration on page 22.

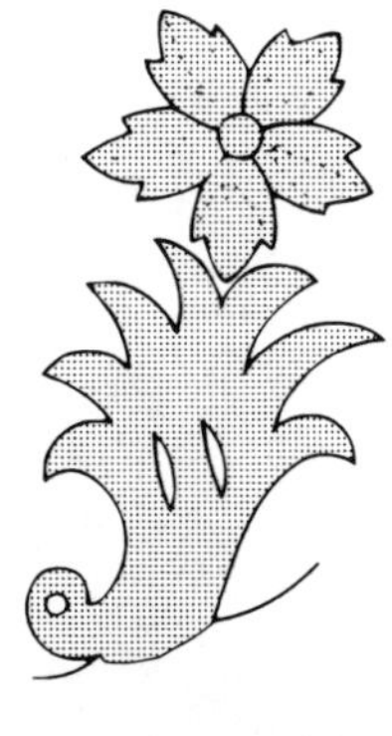

— See finishing and decorating ideas on page 18. —

54

Honeydew Vase with Cantaloupe Flower

— For detailed instructions on use of this stencil see pages 11-12. —

— See illustration on page 21-22 for reference. —

— NOTE —
Broken lines are shown to indicate relief and detail only, and should never be cut through!

I Love You

— Melon Required: Honeydew —

— *For detailed tool usage instructions, see pages 12-15-16-17.* —

1. Prepare melon and stencil for carving using the pattern, tape and X-acto knife. Lightly cut I Love You on melon as described on page 12. Be sure to position pattern about 1-1/2" to 2" off the bottom of melon. Cut base as shown.

2. Using a paring knife and the pattern you have traced as a guide, start to define the I Love You itself, being careful not to detach top, or carve too deeply into the melon. Refer to illustration on page 21.

• Side View •

↖ Base

3. After you are satisfied with your carving, work your way toward the back of the melon until the background arch is flat, (which should be halfway toward the rear of the melon). Do not detach top of carving from melon.

4. Using the V-tool shown above, cut grooves in the background arch to finish your carving. Using a spoon, clean out the inside of the melon.

— *See finishing and decorating ideas on page 18.* —

56

I Love You

— For detailed instructions on use of this stencil see pages 11-12. —

— *See illustration on page 21 for reference.* —

Melon Vase Carvings

— Melons Required: Two Honeydews —

— *For detailed tool usage instructions, see pages 12-15-16-17.* —

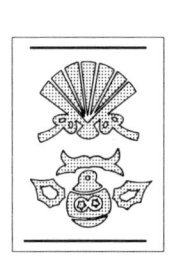

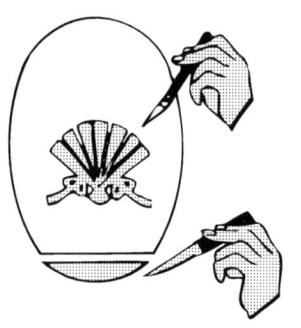

1. Prepare melon and stencils for carving using patterns, tape and X-acto knife. Lightly cut Vase Fan or Christmas Bulb design on melon as described on page 12. Be sure to position pattern about 2 -1/2 inches off the bottom of melon. Cut base as shown.

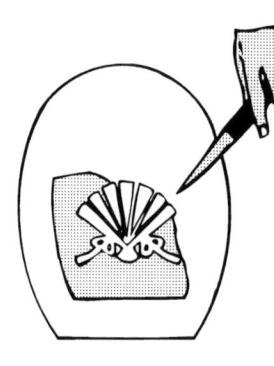

2. Using a paring knife and the pattern you have traced as a guide, start to define the Melon carving itself, being careful not to carve too deeply into the melon. Refer to illustration on page 20. (Only carve the top layer of skin off).

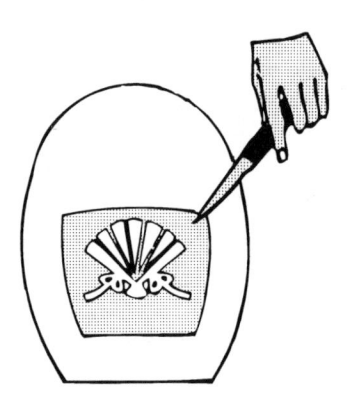

3. After you are satisfied with your carving, work your way outward to create a picture frame around Melon carving. When carving picture frame make sure it is flat.

4. Using the V-tool, cut grooves in the top to make a lid for Melon carving. Using a spoon, clean out the inside of the melon.

— *See finishing and decorating ideas on page 18.* —

Melon Vase Carvings

— For detailed instructions on use of this stencil see pages 11-12. —

— *See illustration on page 20 for reference.* —

Palm Tree

— Melon Required: Honeydew —

— For detailed tool usage instructions, see pages 12-15-16-17. —

1. Prepare melon and stencil for carving using pattern, tape and X-acto knife. Lightly cut Palm Tree design on melon as described on page 12. Be sure to position pattern about 1-1/2" to 2" off the bottom of melon. Cut base as shown.

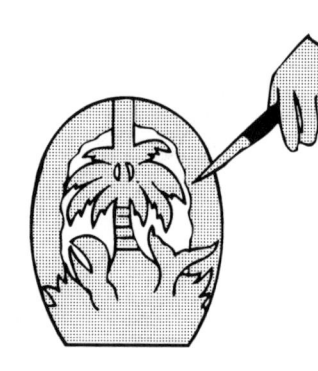

2. Using a paring knife and the pattern you have traced as a guide, start to define the Palm Tree itself, being careful not to detach top, or carve too deeply into the melon. Add detail on broken lines as needed. Refer to illustration on page 21.

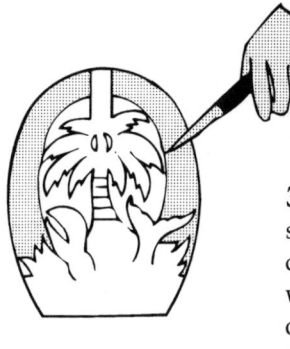

• Side View •

↖ Base

3. After you are satisfied with your carving, work your way toward the back of the melon until the background arch is flat, (which should be halfway toward the rear of the melon). Do not detach top of carving from melon.

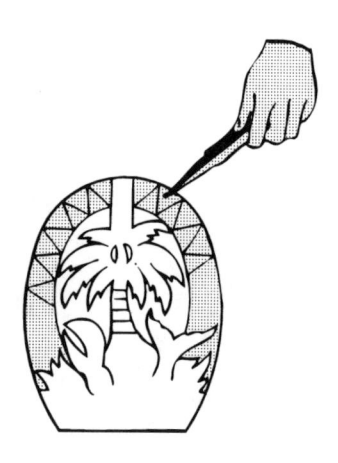

4. Using the V-tool shown above, cut grooves in the background arch to finish your carving. Using a spoon, clean out the inside of the melon.

— See finishing and decorating ideas on page 18. —

60

Palm Tree

— For detailed instructions on use of this stencil see pages 11-12. —

— See illustration on page 21 for reference. —

— NOTE —
Broken lines are shown to indicate relief and detail only, and should never be cut through!

Paradise Fish

— Melons Required: Two Honeydews —

— *For detailed tool usage instructions, see pages 12-15-16-17.* —

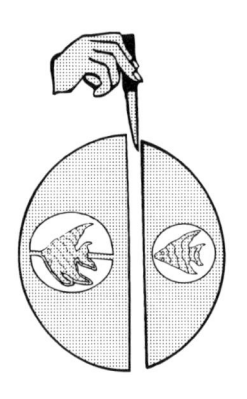

1. Using the 1st melon cut honeydew lengthwise into two sections, other as shown. Remember, you will be carving the Paradise Fish out of the two pieces.

2. Prepare melon sections and stencils for carving using patterns, tape and X-acto knife. Lightly cut Paradise Fish on skin of melon pieces. Using a paring knife and the patterns you have traced as guides, define the Paradise Fish themselves. Add detail on broken lines as needed. Refer to illustration on page 23.

3. Using the 2nd melon, cut honeydew as shown. Remember, you will be attaching the Paradise Fish on this melon.

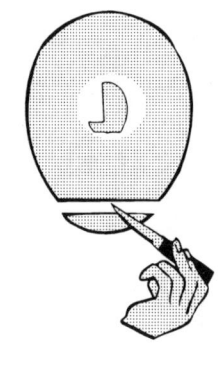

• Side View •

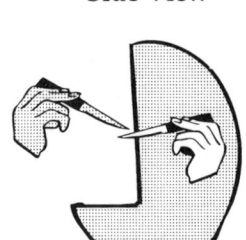

↘ Base

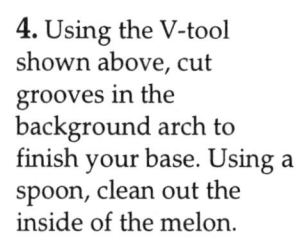

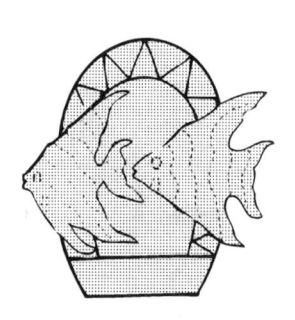

4. Using the V-tool shown above, cut grooves in the background arch to finish your base. Using a spoon, clean out the inside of the melon.

5. Assemble carving with toothpicks, referring to illustration on page 23.

— *See finishing and decorating ideas on page 18.* —

Paradise Fish

— For detailed instructions on use of this stencil see pages 11-12. —

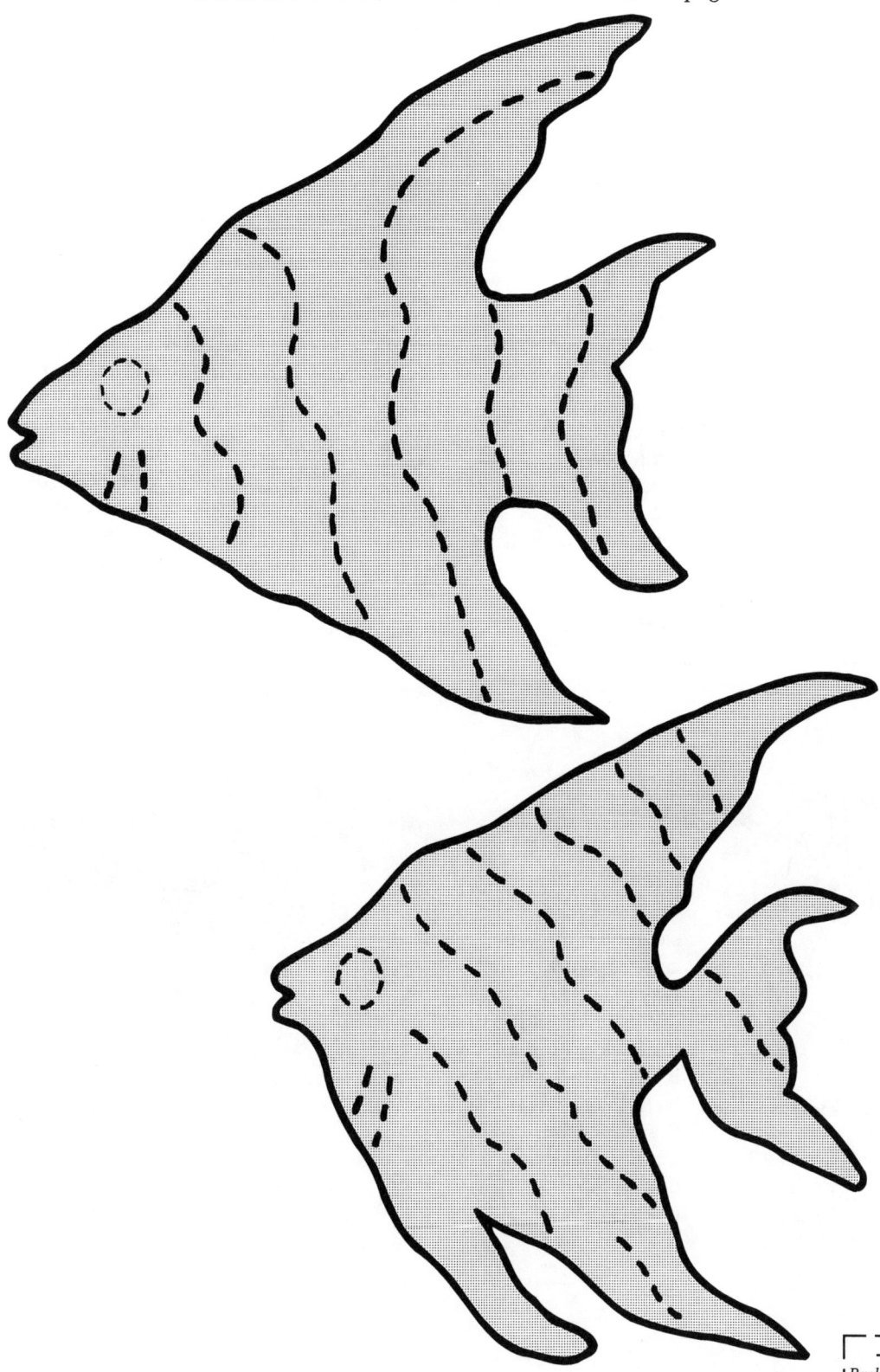

— See illustration on page 23 for reference. —

> — NOTE —
> Broken lines are shown to indicate relief and detail only, and should never be cut through!

Quarter Moon

— Melon Required: Honeydew —

— *For detailed tool usage instructions, see pages 12-15-16-17.* —

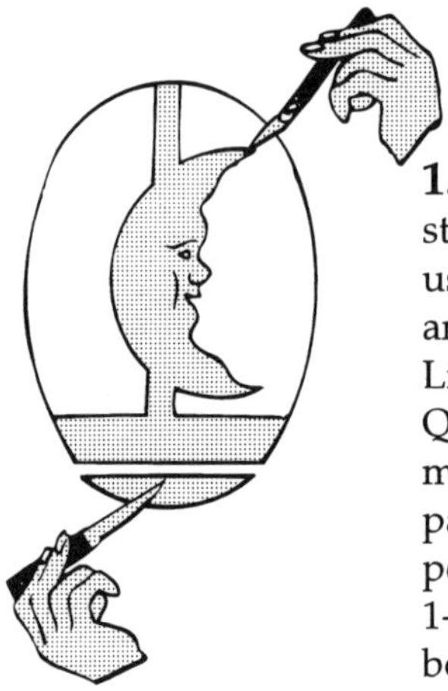

1. Prepare melon and stencil for carving using pattern, tape and X-acto knife. Lightly cut Quarter Moon on melon as described on page 12. Be sure to position pattern about 1-1/2" to 2" off the bottom of melon. Cut base as shown.

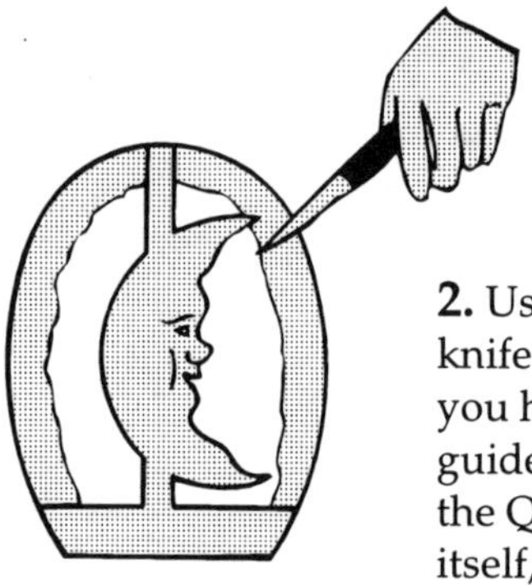

2. Using a paring knife and the pattern you have traced as a guide, start to define the Quarter Moon itself, being careful not to detach top, or carve too deeply into the melon. Refer to illustration on page 21.

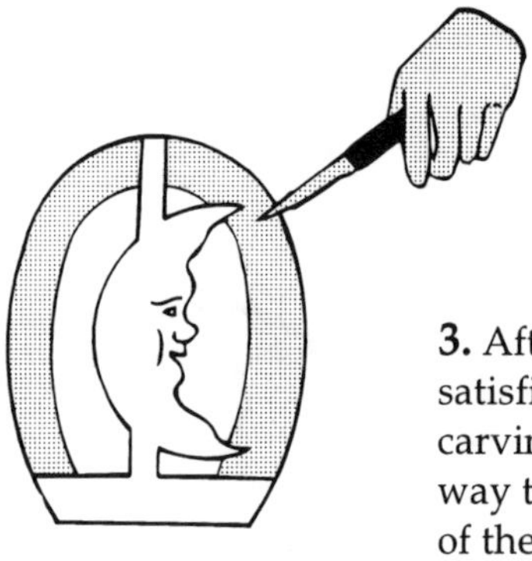

3. After you are satisfied with your carving, work your way toward the back of the melon until the background arch is flat, (which should be halfway toward the rear of the melon). Do not detach top of carving from melon.

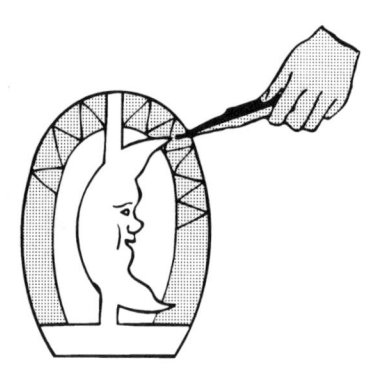

• Side View •

↖ Base

4. Using the V-tool shown above, cut grooves in the background arch to finish your carving. Using a spoon, clean out the inside of the melon.

— *See finishing and decorating ideas on page 18.* —

64

Quarter Moon

— For detailed instructions on use of this stencil see pages 11-12. —

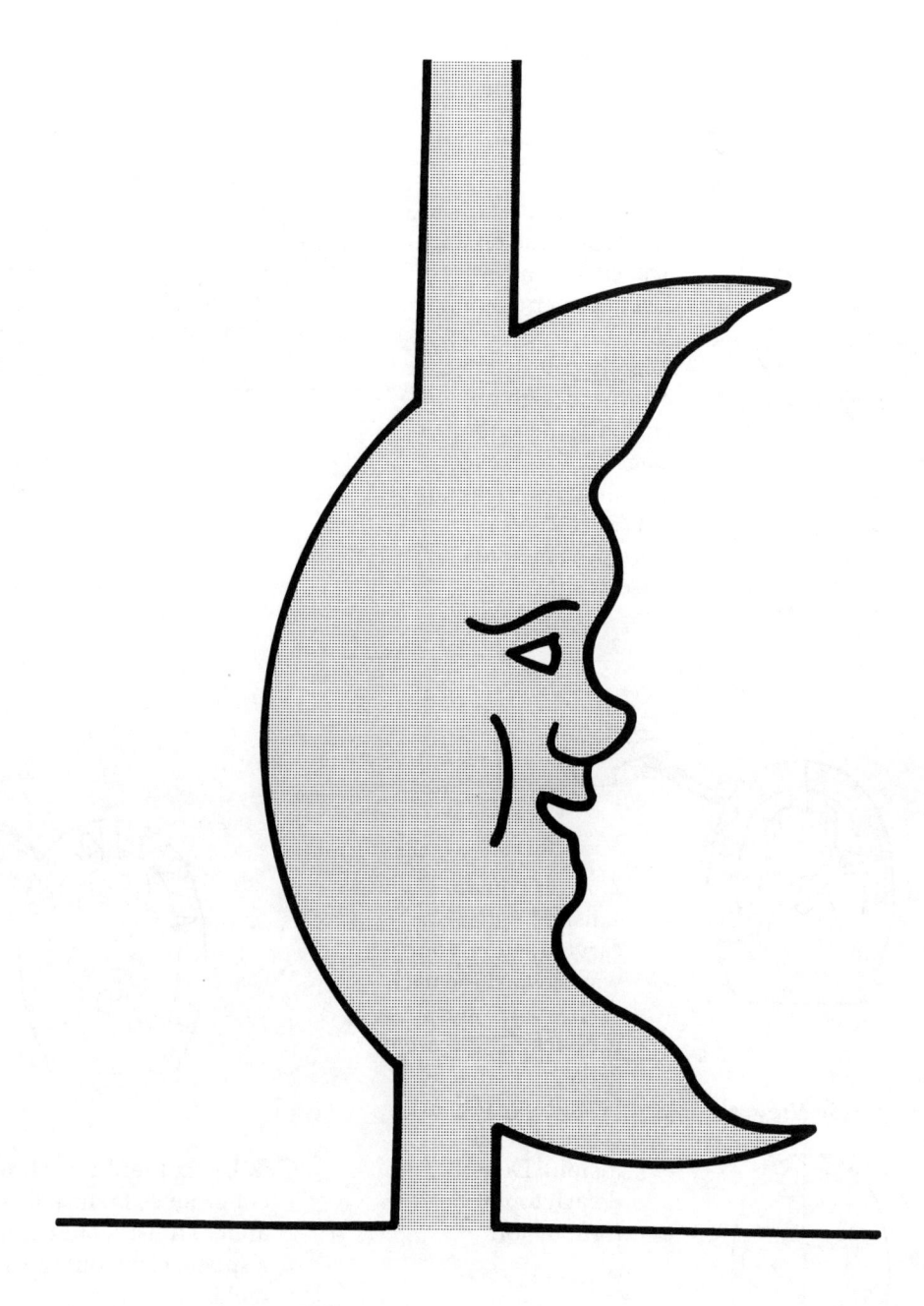

— *See illustration on page 21 for reference.* —

Sailfish

— Melon Required: Honeydew —

— *For detailed tool usage instructions, see pages 12-15-16-17.* —

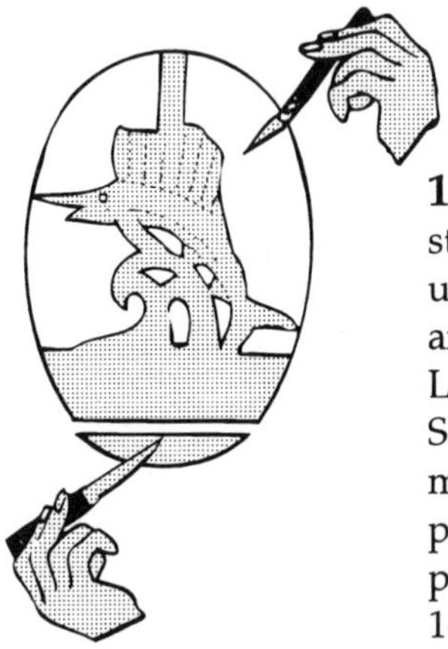

1. Prepare melon and stencil for carving using pattern, tape and X-acto knife. Lightly cut Sailfish design on melon as described on page 12. Be sure to position pattern about 1-1/2" to 2" off the bottom of melon. Cut base as shown.

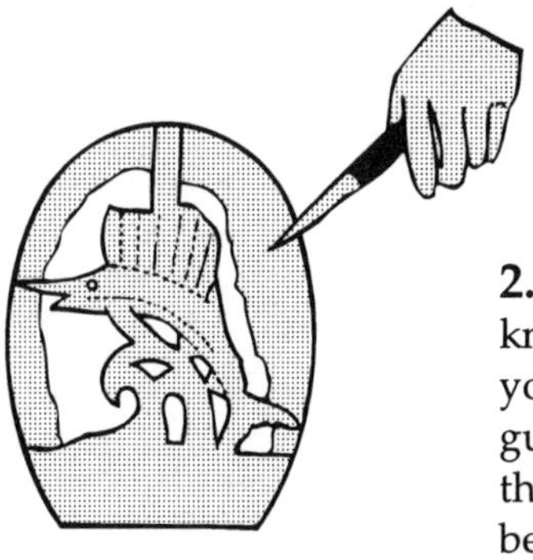

2. Using a paring knife and the pattern you have traced as a guide, start to define the Sailfish itself, being careful not to detach top, or carve too deeply into the melon. Add detail on broken lines as needed. Refer to illustration on page 21.

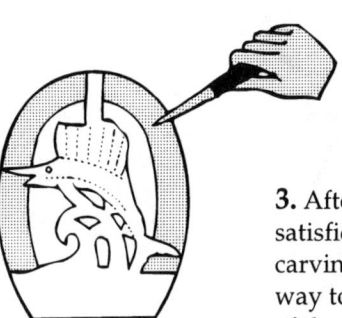

• Side View •

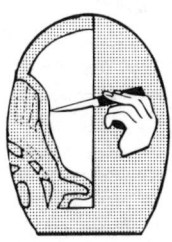

↖ Base

3. After you are satisfied with your carving, work your way toward the back of the melon until the background arch is flat, (which should be halfway toward the rear of the melon). Do not detach top of carving from melon.

4. Using the V-tool shown above, cut grooves in the background arch to finish your carving. Using a spoon, clean out the inside of the melon.

— *See finishing and decorating ideas on page 18.* —

Sailfish

— For detailed instructions on use of this stencil see pages 11-12. —

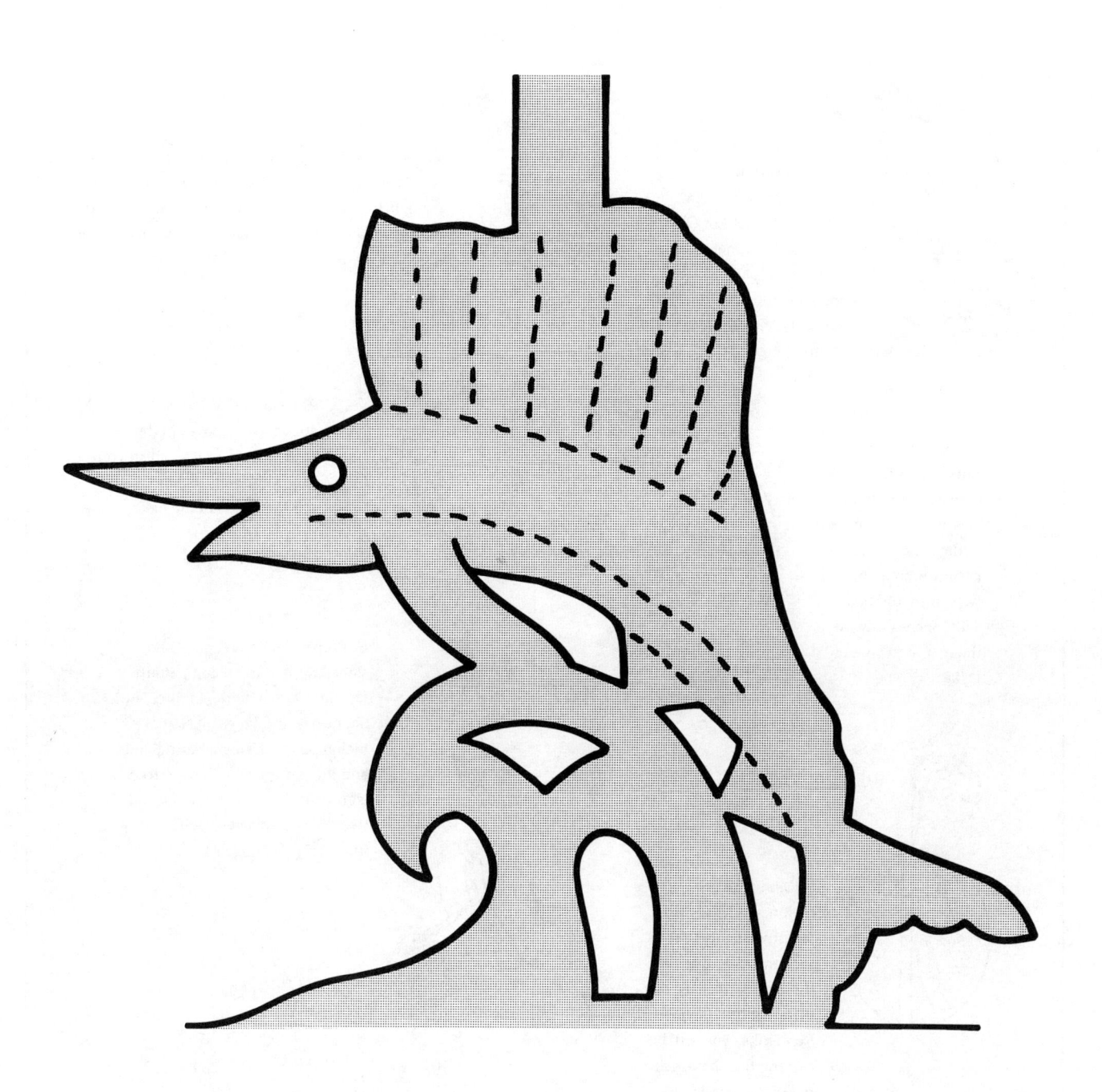

— *See illustration on page 21 for reference.* —

— NOTE —
Broken lines are shown to indicate relief and detail only, and should never be cut through!

St. Patrick's Shamrock and Pot O' Gold

— Melons Required: Two Honeydews —

— *For detailed tool usage instructions, see pages 12-15-16-17.* —

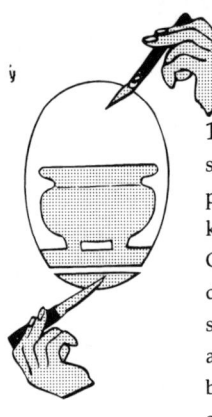

1. Prepare 1st melon and stencil for carving using pattern, tape and X-acto knife. Lightly cut Pot O' Gold design on melon as described on page 12. Be sure to position pattern about 1-1/2" to 2" off the bottom of melon. Cut base as shown.

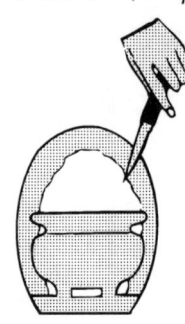

2. Using a paring knife and the pattern you have traced as a guide, start to define the Pot O' Gold itself, being careful not to carve too deeply into the melon. Add detail on broken line as needed. Refer to illustrations on pages 21 and 24.

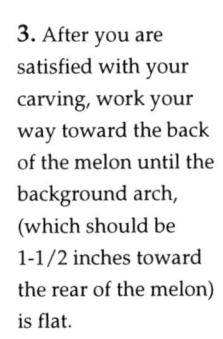

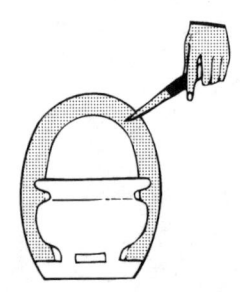

3. After you are satisfied with your carving, work your way toward the back of the melon until the background arch, (which should be 1-1/2 inches toward the rear of the melon) is flat.

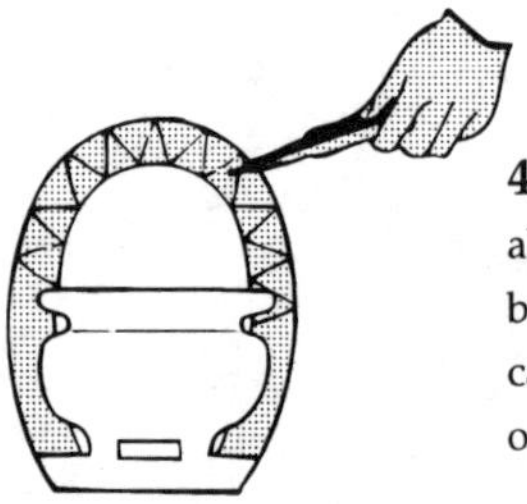

4. Using the V-tool shown above, cut grooves in the background arch to finish your carving. Using a spoon, clean out the inside of the melon.

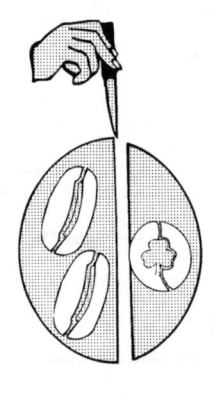

5. Using the 2nd melon, cut honeydew lengthwise into two sections, one roughly three times the size of the other as shown. Remember you will be carving the Shamrock out of the small piece and using the large piece for carving the two Poles.

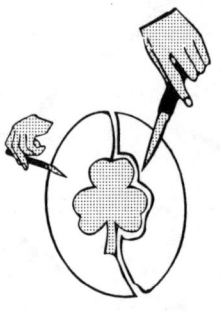

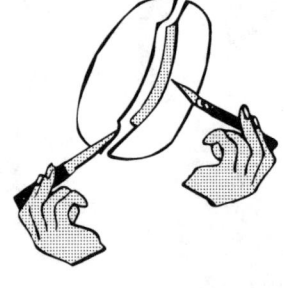

6. Prepare melon sections and stencil for carving using pattern, tape and X-acto knife. Lightly cut Shamrock and Poles on skin of melon pieces. Using a paring knife and the patterns you have traced as a guide define the Shamrock and two Poles themselves. Refer to illustration on page 24.

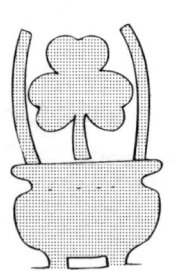

7. Assemble carving with toothpicks, referring to illustration.

— *See finishing and decorating ideas on page 18.* —

St. Patrick's Shamrock and Pot O'Gold

— For detailed instructions on use of this stencil see pages 11-12. —

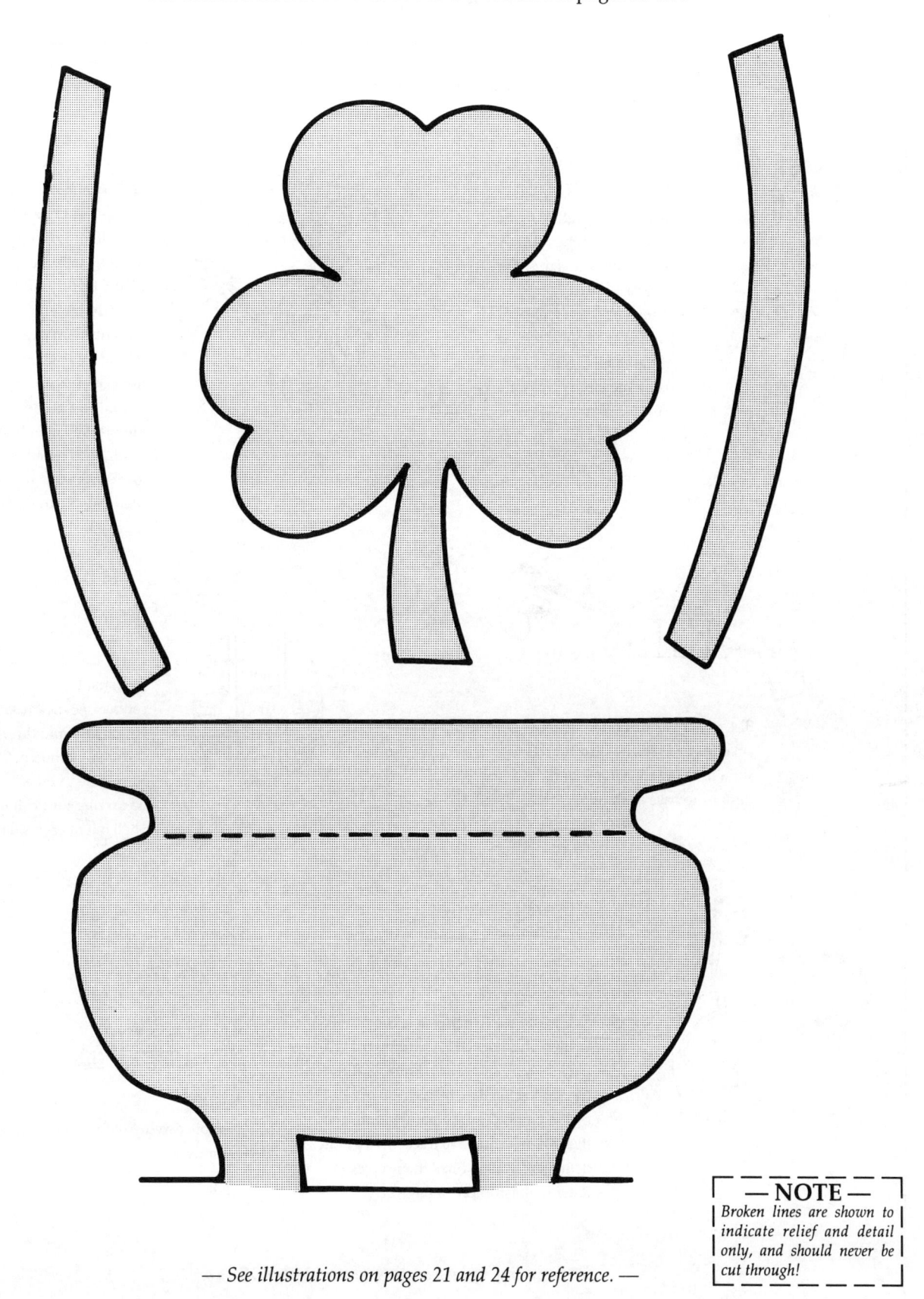

— See illustrations on pages 21 and 24 for reference. —

— NOTE —
Broken lines are shown to indicate relief and detail only, and should never be cut through!

Scallop Shell and Palm Tree

— Melons Required: Honeydew and Cantaloupe —

— *For detailed tool usage instructions, see pages 12-15-16-17.* —

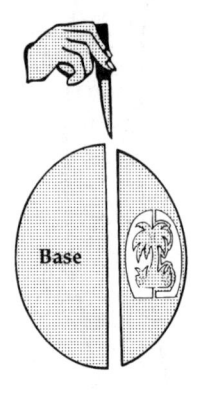

1. Using the honeydew melon, cut lengthwise into two sections, one roughly three times the size of the other as shown. Remember, you will be carving the Palm Tree out of the small piece and using the large piece for a base.

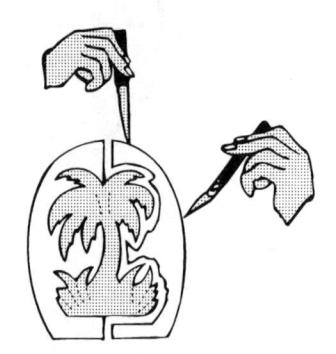

2. Prepare small melon section and Palm Tree stencil for carving using pattern, tape and X-acto knife. Lightly cut Palm Tree design on melon as described on page 12. Using a paring knife and the pattern you have traced as a guide, start to define the Palm Tree itself. Add detail on broken lines as needed. Refer to illustration on page 23.

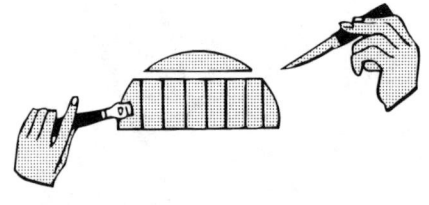

3. Using a paring knife, cut off a small piece of the base section, as shown. Using a Channel knife, add designs to base as shown.

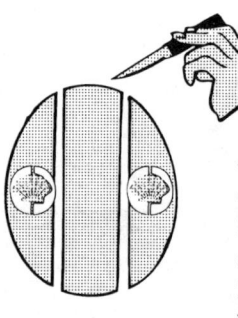

4. Using the cantaloupe melon, cut lengthwise into three sections, as shown. Remember, you will be carving the Scallop Shell out of each side piece.

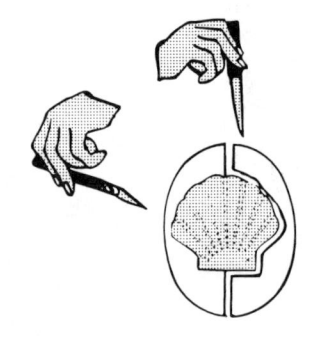

5. Prepare the two melon sections and Scallop Shell stencil for carving using pattern, tape and X-acto knife. Lightly cut Scallop Shell on inside skin of melon pieces. Using a paring knife and the patterns you have traced as a guide define the Scallop Shell themselves. Refer to illustration on page 22.

6. Assemble carving with toothpicks, referring to illustrations.

— *See finishing and decorating ideas on page 18.* —

70

Scallop Shell and Palm Tree

— For detailed instructions on use of this stencil see pages 11-12. —

— See illustration on pages 22-23 for reference. —

```
— NOTE —
Broken lines are shown to
indicate relief and detail
only, and should never be
cut through!
```

Seahorse with Seaweed

— Melons Required: Honeydew and Cantaloupe —

— For detailed tool usage instructions, see pages 12-15-16-17. —

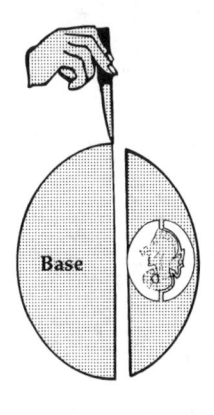

1. Using the honeydew melon, cut lengthwise into two sections, one roughly three times the size of the other as shown. Remember, you will be carving the Seahorse out of the small piece and using the large piece for a base.

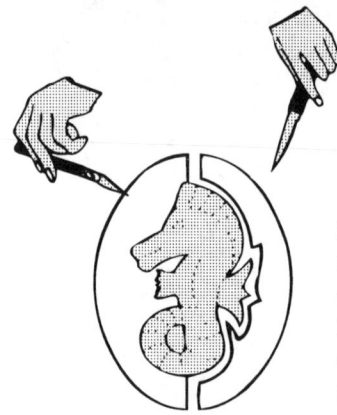

2. Prepare small melon section and Seahorse stencil for carving using pattern, tape and X-acto knife. Lightly cut Seahorse design on melon as described on page 12. Using a paring knife and the pattern you have traced as a guide, start to define the Seahorse itself. Add detail on broken lines as needed. Refer to illustration on page 23.

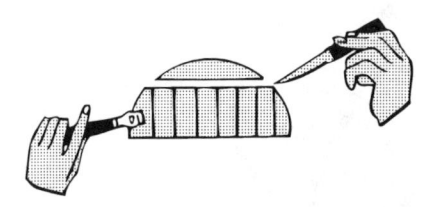

3. Using a paring knife, cut off a small piece of the base section, as shown. Using a Channel knife, add design to base as shown. Refer to illustration on page 23.

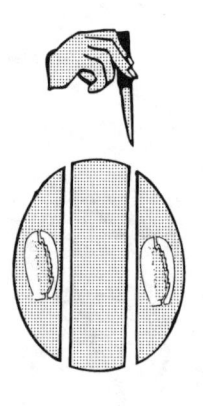

4. Using the cantaloupe melon, cut lengthwise into three sections, as shown. Remember, you will be carving the Seaweed out of each side piece.

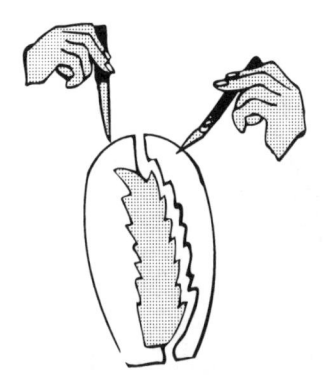

5. Prepare the two melon sections and Seaweed stencil for carving using pattern, tape and X-acto knife. Lightly cut Seaweed on inside skin of melon pieces. Using a paring knife and the patterns you have traced as a guide define the Seaweed themselves. Refer to illustration on page 22.

6. Assemble carving with toothpicks, referring to illustration.

— See finishing and decorating ideas on page 18. —

Seahorse with Seaweed

— For detailed instructions on use of this stencil see pages 11-12. —

— See illustration on page 23 for reference. —

— NOTE —
Broken lines are shown to indicate relief and detail only, and should never be cut through!

Seal with Ball

— Melon Required: Honeydew —

— *For detailed tool usage instructions, see pages 12-15-16-17.* —

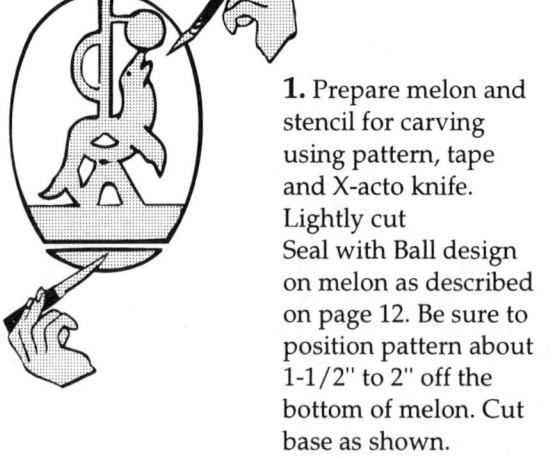

1. Prepare melon and stencil for carving using pattern, tape and X-acto knife. Lightly cut Seal with Ball design on melon as described on page 12. Be sure to position pattern about 1-1/2" to 2" off the bottom of melon. Cut base as shown.

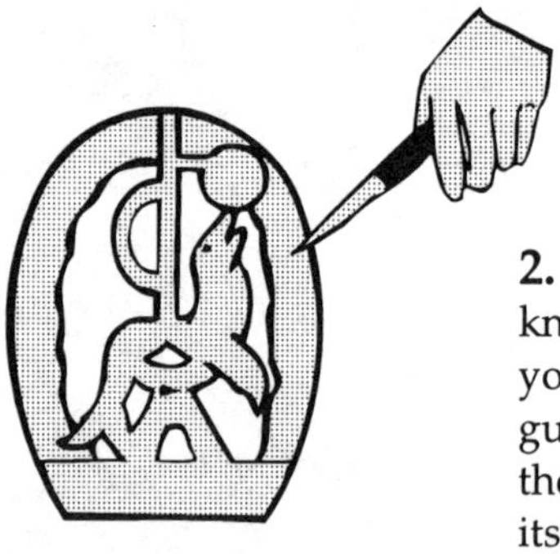

2. Using a paring knife and the pattern you have traced as a guide, start to define the Seal with Ball itself, being careful not to detach top, or carve too deeply into the melon. Add detail on broken lines as needed. Refer to illustrations on page 21.

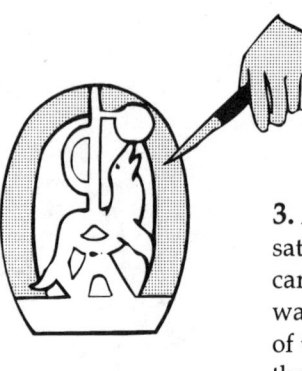

3. After you are satisfied with your carving, work your way toward the back of the melon until the background arch is flat, (which should be halfway toward the rear of the melon). Do not detach top of carving from melon.

• Side View •

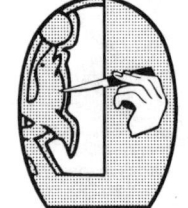

↖ Base

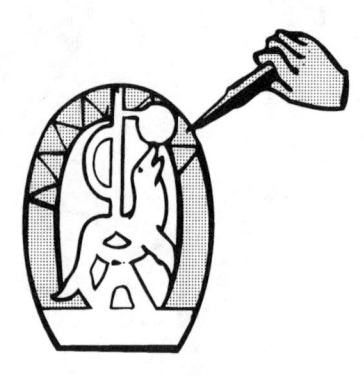

4. Using the V-tool shown above, cut grooves in the background arch to finish your carving. Using a spoon, clean out the inside of the melon.

— *See finishing and decorating ideas on page 18.* —

74

Seal with Ball

— For detailed instructions on use of this stencil see pages 11-12. —

— See illustrations on page 21 for references. —

— NOTE —
Broken lines are shown to indicate relief and detail only, and should never be cut through!

Southwestern Cactus Carving

— Melon Required: Honeydew —

— *For detailed tool usage instructions, see pages 12-15-16-17.* —

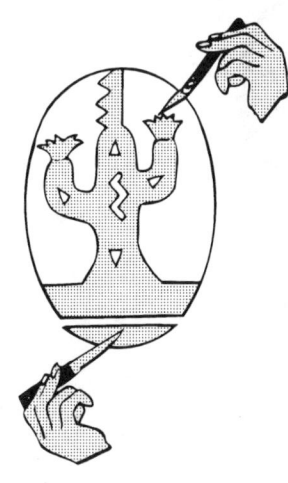

1. Prepare melon and stencil for carving using pattern, tape and X-acto knife. Lightly cut Southwestern Cactus design on melon as described on page 12. Be sure to position pattern about 1-1/2" to 2" off the bottom of melon. Cut base as shown.

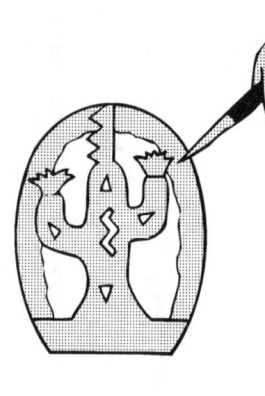

2. Using a paring knife and the pattern you have traced as a guide, start to define the Cactus itself, being careful not to detach top, or carve too deeply into the melon. Add detail on broken lines as needed. Refer to illustration on page 21.

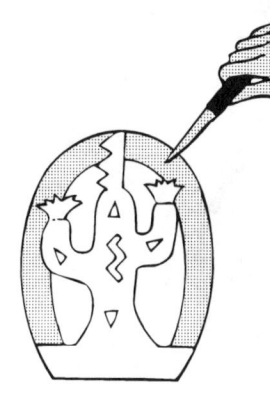

3. After you are satisfied with your carving, work your way toward the back of the melon until the background arch is flat, (which should be halfway toward the rear of the melon). Do not detach top of carving from melon.

• Side View •

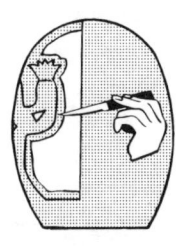

↖ Base

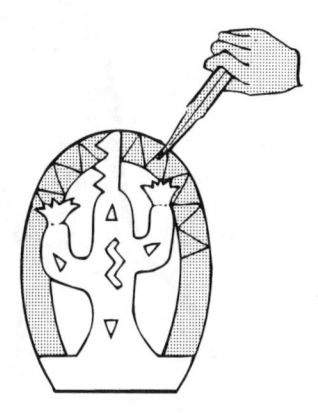

4. Using the V-tool shown above, cut grooves in the background arch to finish your carving. Using a spoon, clean out the inside of the melon.

— *See finishing and decorating ideas on page 18.* —

Southwestern Cactus Carving

— For detailed instructions on use of this stencil see pages 11-12. —

— See illustration on page 21 for reference. —

— NOTE —
Broken lines are shown to indicate relief and detail only, and should never be cut through!

Southwestern Coyote Carving

— Melon Required: Honeydew —

— *For detailed tool usage instructions, see pages 12-15-16-17.* —

1. Prepare melon and stencil for carving using pattern, tape and X-acto knife. Lightly cut Southwestern Coyote design on melon as described on page 12. Be sure to position pattern about 1-1/2" to 2" off the bottom of melon. Cut base as shown.

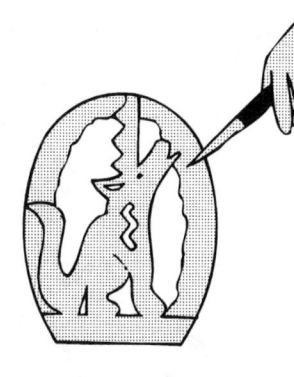

2. Using a paring knife and the pattern you have traced as a guide, start to define the Coyote itself, being careful not to detach top, or carve too deeply into the melon. Add detail on broken lines as needed. Refer to illustration on page 21.

3. After you are satisfied with your carving, work your way toward the back of the melon until the background arch is flat, (which should be halfway toward the rear of the melon). Do not detach top of carving from melon.

• Side View •

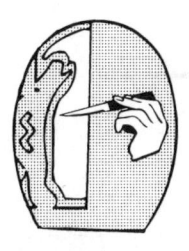

↖ Base

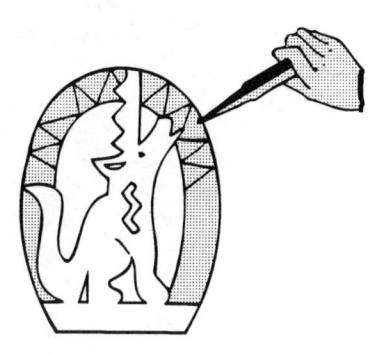

4. Using the V-tool shown above, cut grooves in the background arch to finish your carving. Using a spoon, clean out the inside of the melon.

— *See finishing and decorating ideas on page 18.* —

78

Southwestern Coyote Carving

— For detailed instructions on use of this stencil see pages 11-12. —

— See illustration on page 21 for reference. —

— NOTE —
Broken lines are shown to indicate relief and detail only, and should never be cut through!

Star of David

— Melon Required: Honeydew —

— *For detailed tool usage instructions, see pages 12-15-16-17.* —

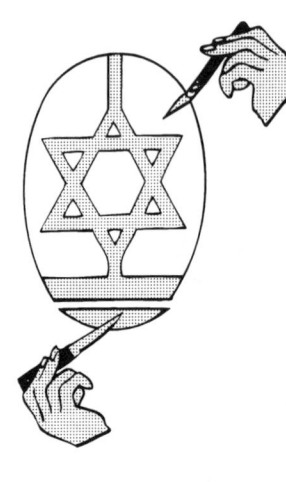

1. Prepare melon and stencil for carving using pattern, tape and X-acto knife. Lightly cut Star of David on melon as described on page 12. Be sure to position pattern about 1-1/2" to 2" off the bottom of melon. Cut base as shown.

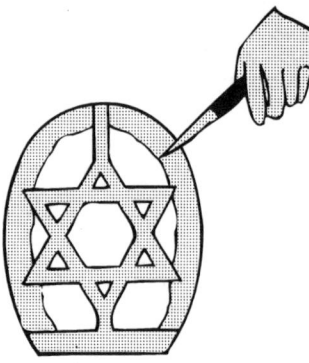

2. Using the pattern you have traced as a guide, start to define the Star of David itself, being careful not to detach top, or carve too deeply into the melon. Refer to illustration on page 21.

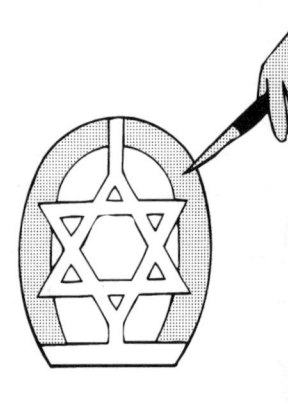

• Side View •

↘ Base

3. After you are satisfied with your carving, work your way toward the back of the melon until the background arch is flat, (which should be halfway toward the rear of the melon). Do not detach top of carving from melon.

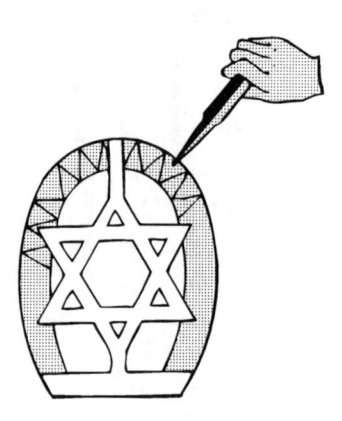

4. Using the V-tool shown above, cut grooves in the background arch to finish your carving. Using a spoon, clean out the inside of the melon.

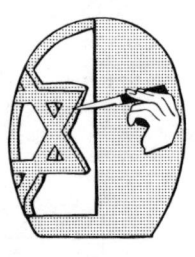

— *See finishing and decorating ideas on page 18.* —

80

Star of David

— For detailed instructions on use of this stencil see pages 11-12. —

— *See illustration on page 21 for reference.* —

Swordfish with Banners

— Melons Required: Honeydew and Cantaloupe —

— *For detailed tool usage instructions, see pages 12-15-16-17.* —

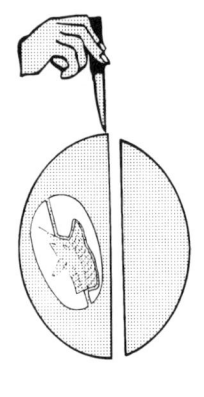

1. Using the honeydew melon, cut lengthwise into two sections, one roughly three times the size of the other as shown. Remember, you will be carving the Swordfish out of the large section. Small piece is extra.

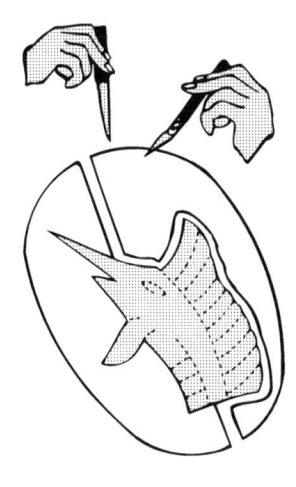

2. Prepare large melon section and Swordfish stencil for carving using pattern, tape and X-acto knife. Lightly cut Swordfish design on melon as described on page 12. Using a paring knife and the pattern you have traced as a guide, start to define the Swordfish itself. Add detail on broken lines as needed. Refer to illustration on page 23.

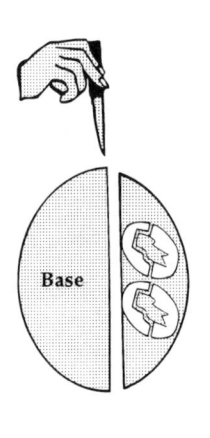

3. Using the cantaloupe melon, cut lengthwise into two sections, as shown. Remember, you will be carving the Banners out of the small piece with the large piece being used for a base.

4. Prepare the small melon section and Banner stencils for carving using pattern, tape and X-acto knife. Lightly cut Banners on inside flesh of melon piece. Using a paring knife and the patterns you have traced as a guide define the Banners themselves. Refer to illustration on page 22.

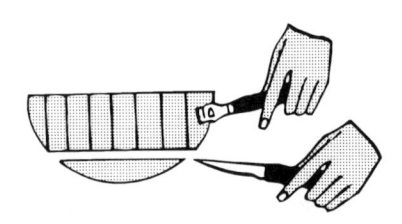

5. Using a paring knife, cut off a small piece of the base section, as shown. Using a Channel knife, add design to base as shown.

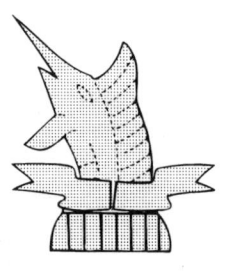

6. Assemble carving with toothpicks, referring to illustrations.

— *See finishing and decorating ideas on page 18.* —

Swordfish with Banners

— For detailed instructions on use of this stencil see pages 11-12. —

— See illustrations on pages 22-23 for references.—

— NOTE —
Broken lines are shown to indicate relief and detail only, and should never be cut through!

Tropical Bird

— Melons Required: Two Honeydews —

— *For detailed tool usage instructions, see pages 12-15-16-17.* —

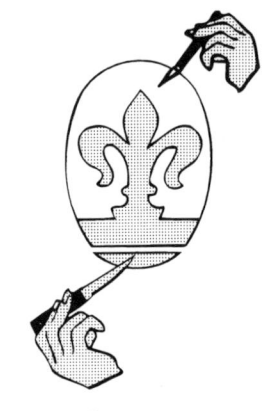

1. Prepare 1st melon and stencil carving using pattern, tape and X-acto knife. Lightly cut Saint design on melon as described on page 12. Be sure to position pattern about 1-1/2" to 2" off the bottom of melon. Cut base as shown.

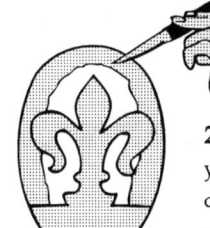

2. Using a paring knife and the pattern you have traced as a guide, start to define the Saint design itself, being careful not to carve too deeply into the melon. Refer to illustration on page 21.

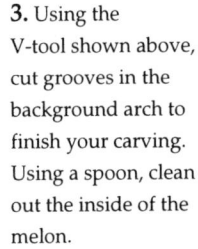

3. Using the V-tool shown above, cut grooves in the background arch to finish your carving. Using a spoon, clean out the inside of the melon.

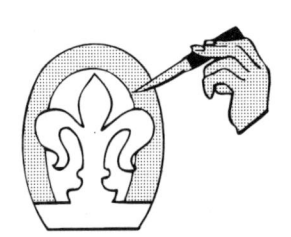

3. After you are satisfied with your carving, work your way toward the back of the melon until the background arch, (which should be halfway toward the rear of the melon) is flat.

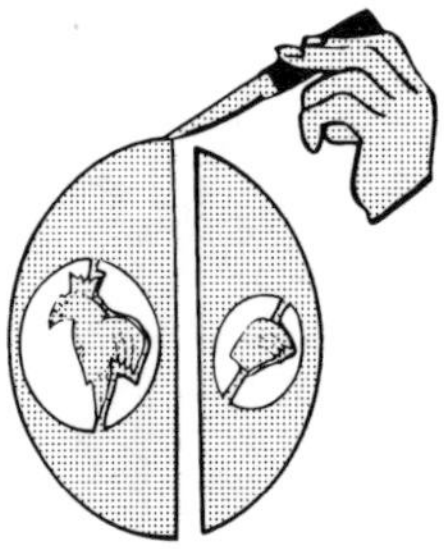

4. Using the 2nd honeydew melon, cut lengthwise into two sections, as shown. Remember, you will be carving the Tropical Bird out of large piece. Carving the Wing out of small piece.

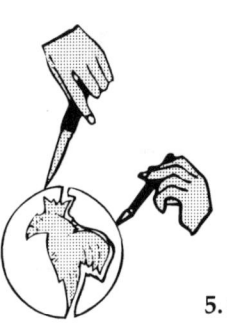

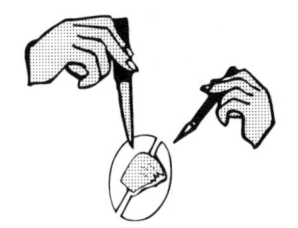

5. Prepare melon sections, Tropical Bird and Wing stencils, for carving using patterns, tape and X-acto knife. Lightly cut Tropical Bird and Wing designs on melon sections as described on page 12. Using a paring knife and the pattern you have traced as a guide, start to define the Tropical Bird and Wing themselves. Add detail on broken lines as needed. Refer to illustrations on page 24 and front cover.

6. Assemble carving with toothpicks, referring to illustration.

— *See finishing and decorating ideas on page 18.* —

84

Tropical Bird

— For detailed instructions on use of this stencil see pages 11-12. —

— NOTE —
Broken lines are shown to indicate relief and detail only, and should never be cut through!

— *See illustrations on pages 21, 24 and front cover for references.* —

Vase

— Melon Required: Honeydew —

— For detailed tool usage instructions, see pages 12-15-16-17. —

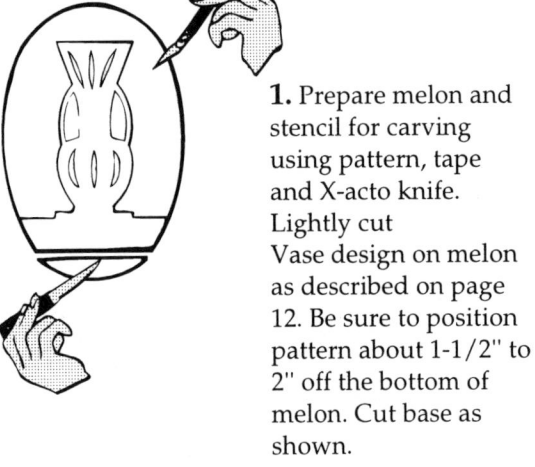

1. Prepare melon and stencil for carving using pattern, tape and X-acto knife. Lightly cut Vase design on melon as described on page 12. Be sure to position pattern about 1-1/2" to 2" off the bottom of melon. Cut base as shown.

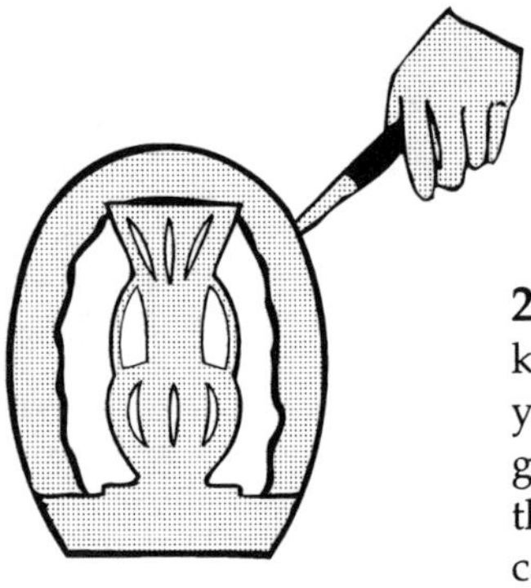

2. Using a paring knife and the pattern you have traced as a guide, start to define the Vase itself, being careful not to carve too deeply into the melon. Refer to illustration on page 21.

• Side View •

↖ Base

3. After you are satisfied with your carving, work your way toward the back of the melon until the background arch is flat, (which should be halfway toward the rear of the melon).

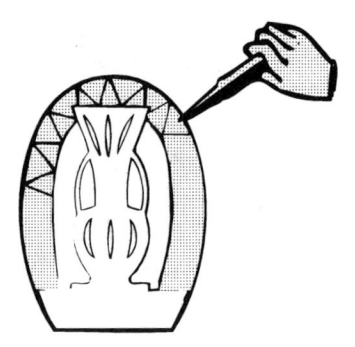

4. Using the V-tool shown above, cut grooves in the background arch to finish your carving. Using a spoon, clean out the inside of the melon.

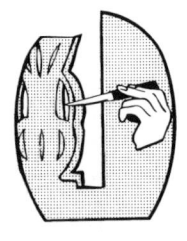

— See finishing and decorating ideas on page 18. —

86

Vase

— For detailed instructions on use of this stencil see pages 11-12. —

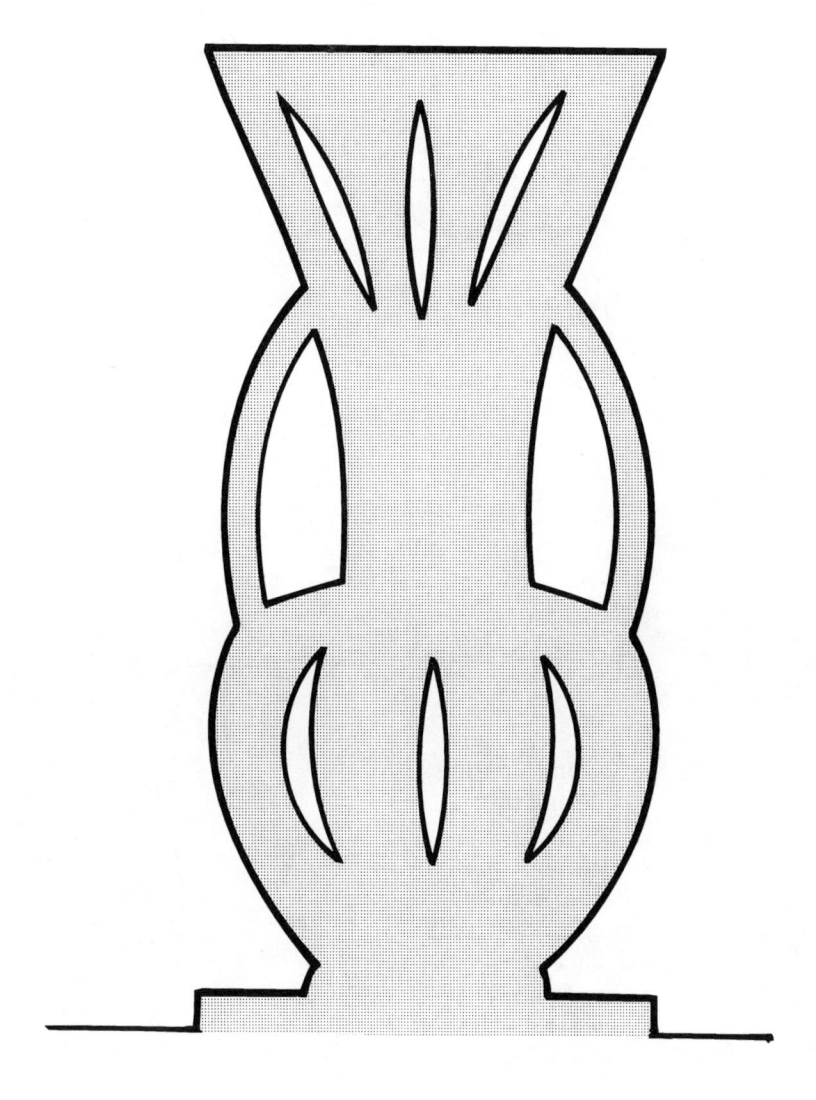

— *See illustration on page 21 for reference.* —

Honeydew Dragon

—Melon Required: Honeydew—

— *For detailed tool usage instructions, see pages 12-15-16-17.* —

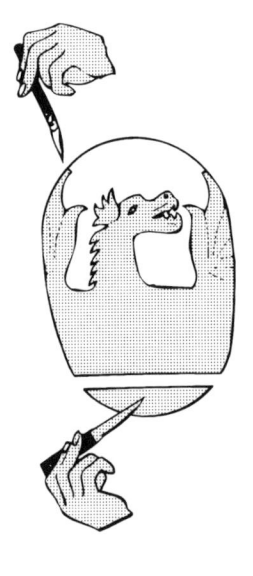

1. Prepare melon and stencils for carving using patterns, tape and X-acto knife.

Lightly cut Dragon Head, Wings and Tail, designs on melon as described on page 12. Be sure to position patterns about 1-1/2" to 2" off the bottom of melon.

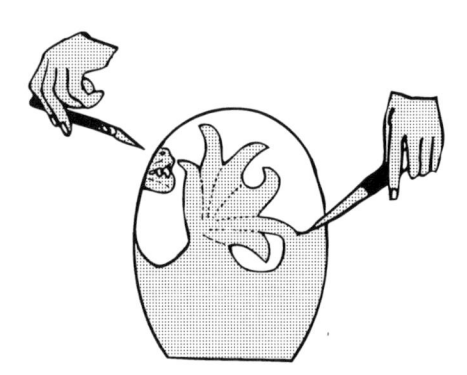

2. Be sure to layout Dragon designs on melon so the Head, Wings and Tail, are positioned in the right place. Cut base as shown.

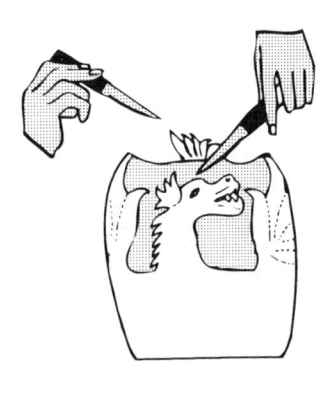

3. Using a paring knife and the patterns you have traced as a guide, start to define the Dragon itself. Add detail on broken lines as needed. Refer to illustration on page 24.

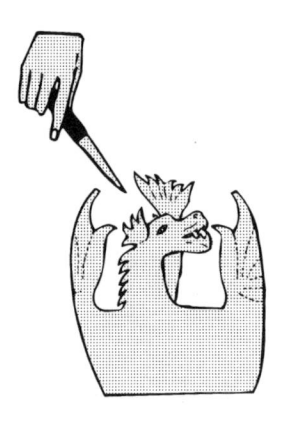

4. After you are satisfied with your Dragon carving, using a spoon, clean out the inside of the melon.

— *See finishing and decorating ideas on page 18.* —

Honeydew Dragon

— For detailed instructions on use of this stencil see pages 11-12. —

— See illustration on page 24 for reference.—

— NOTE —
Broken lines are shown to indicate relief and detail only, and should never be cut through!

Honeydew Dragon

— *For detailed instructions on use of this stencil see pages 11-12.* —

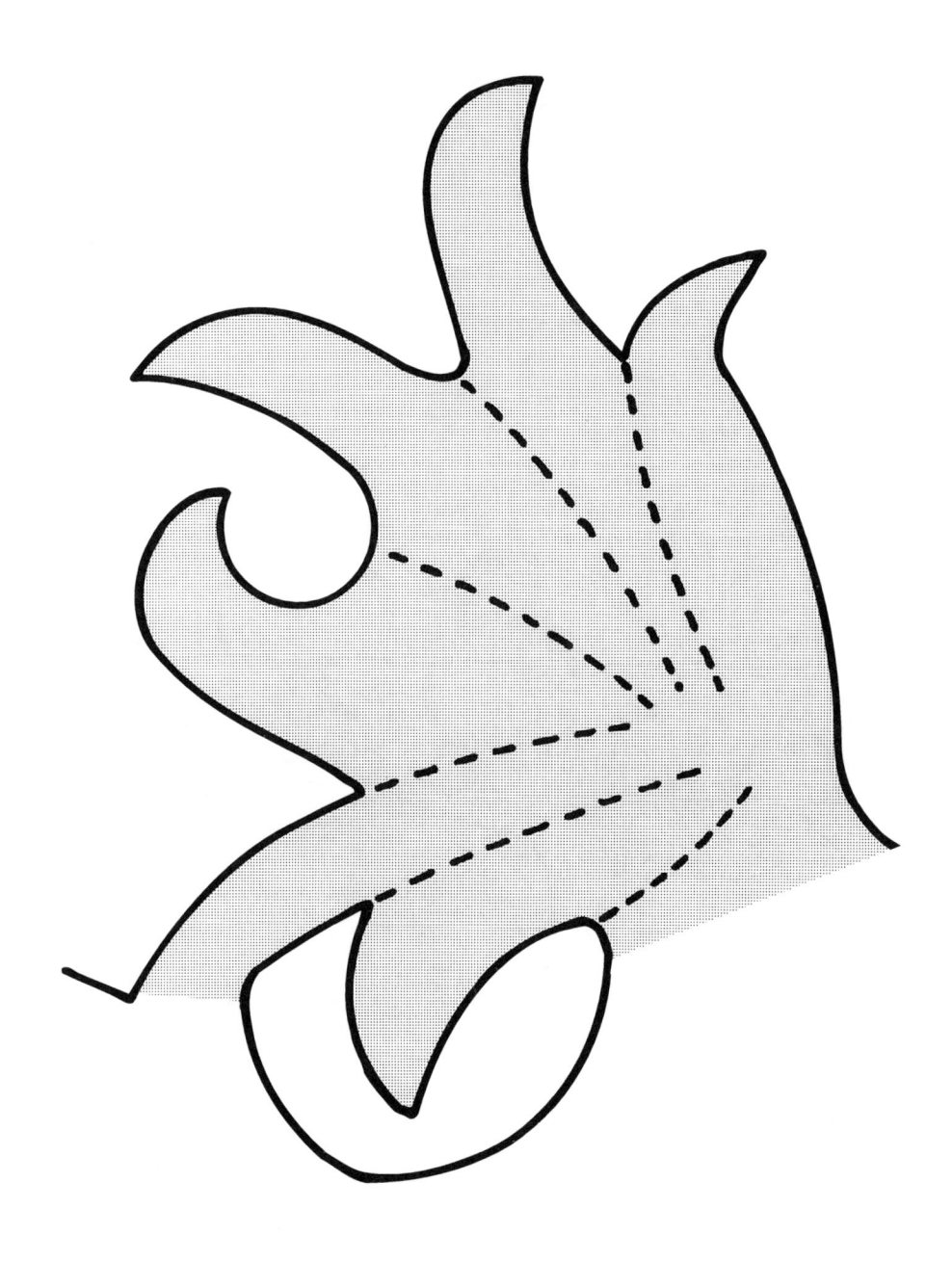

—*See illustration on page 24 for reference.*—

—NOTE—
Broken lines are shown to indicate relief and detail only, and should never be cut through!

Honeydew Dragon

— For detailed instructions on use of this stencil see pages 11-12. —

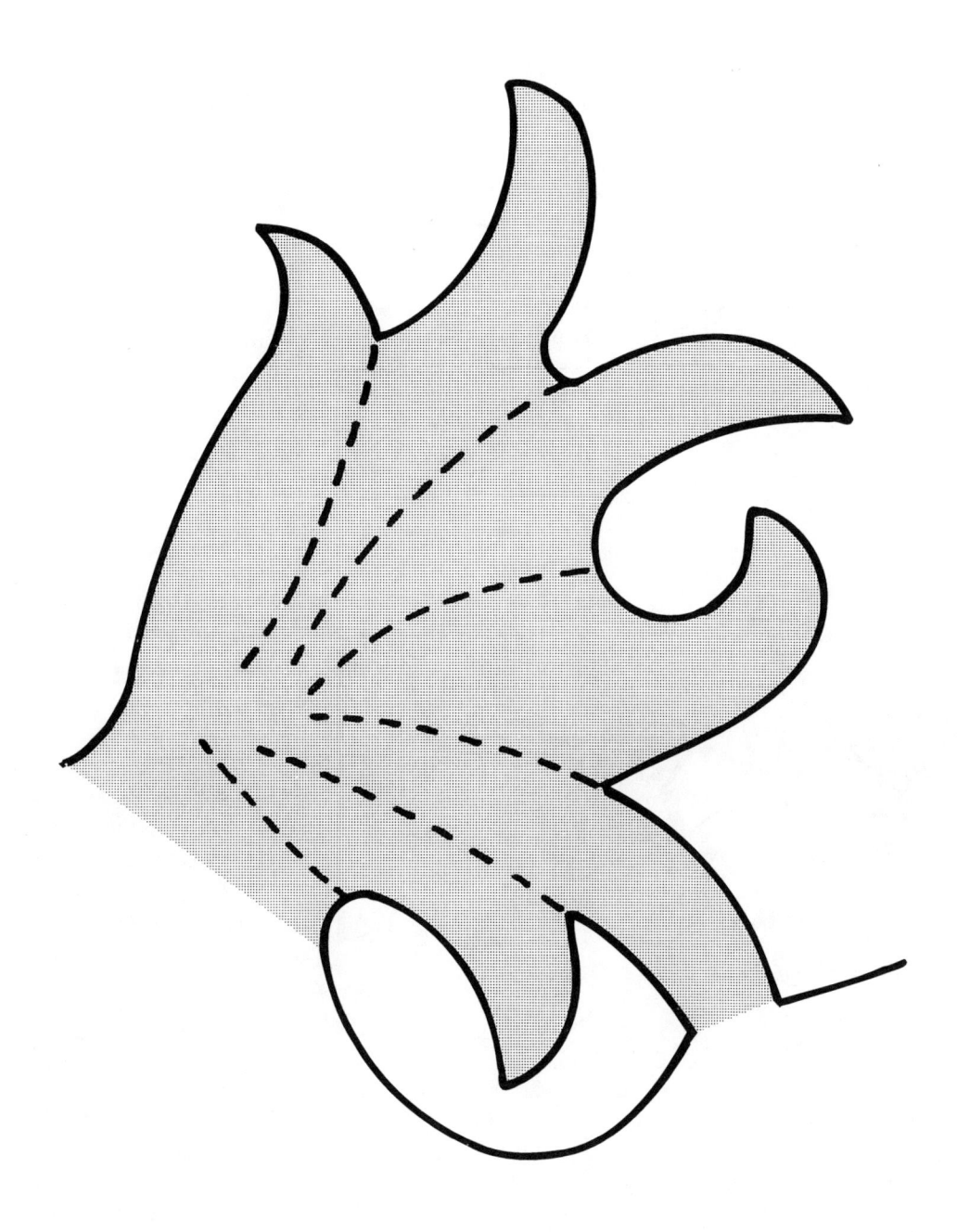

— See illustration on page 24 for reference.—

— NOTE —
Broken lines are shown to indicate relief and detail only, and should never be cut through!

Swan I

—Melons Required: Two Honeydews—

— *For detailed tool usage instructions, see pages 12-15-16-17.* —

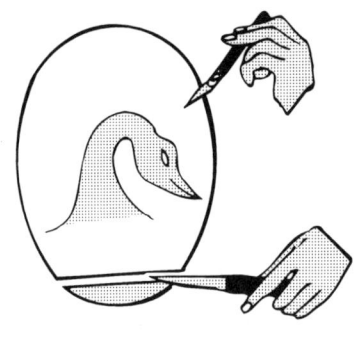

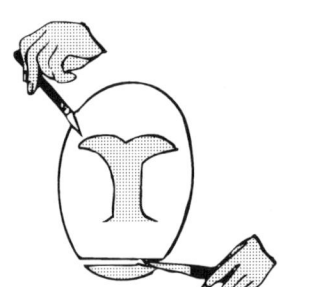

1. Prepare first melon and stencils for carving using patterns, tape and X-acto knife. Lightly cut Swan Head and Tail as described on page 12. Be sure to position pattern about 1-1/2" to 2" off the bottom of melon. Cut base as shown. (Make sure you align properly as shown).

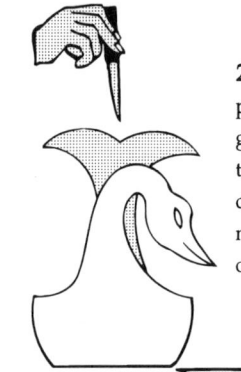

2. Using the Head and Tail pattern you have traced as a guide, start to define part of the Swan I body itself. Add detail on broken lines as needed. Refer to illustration on page 24.

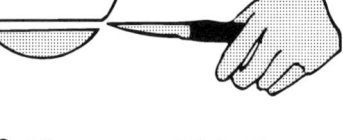

3. After you are satisfied with the wing and tail carving, use a spoon and clean out the inside of the melon.

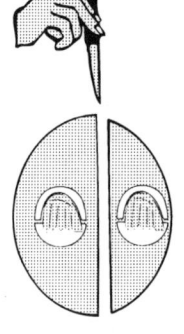

4. Using the 2nd melon, cut honeydew lengthwise into two sections, as shown. Remember, you will be carving the Swan Wings out of each piece.

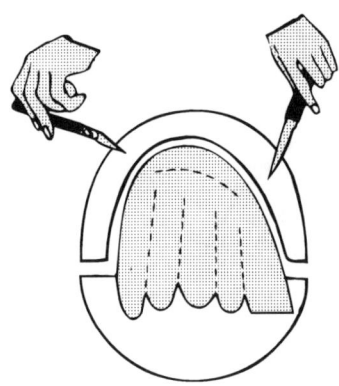

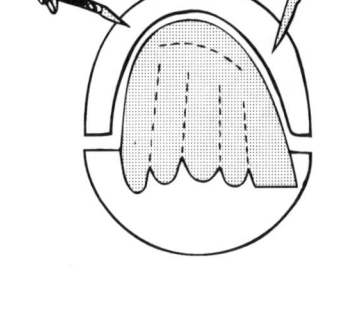

5. Prepare melon sections and stencils for carving using patterns, tape and X-acto knife. Lightly cut Swan I Wings on skin of melon pieces. Using the patterns you have traced as a guide and a paring knife define the Swan Wings themselves. Refer to illustration on page 24.

6. Assemble carving with toothpicks, referring to illustration.

— *See finishing and decorating ideas on page 18.* —

Swan I

— For detailed instructions on use of this stencil see pages 11-12. —

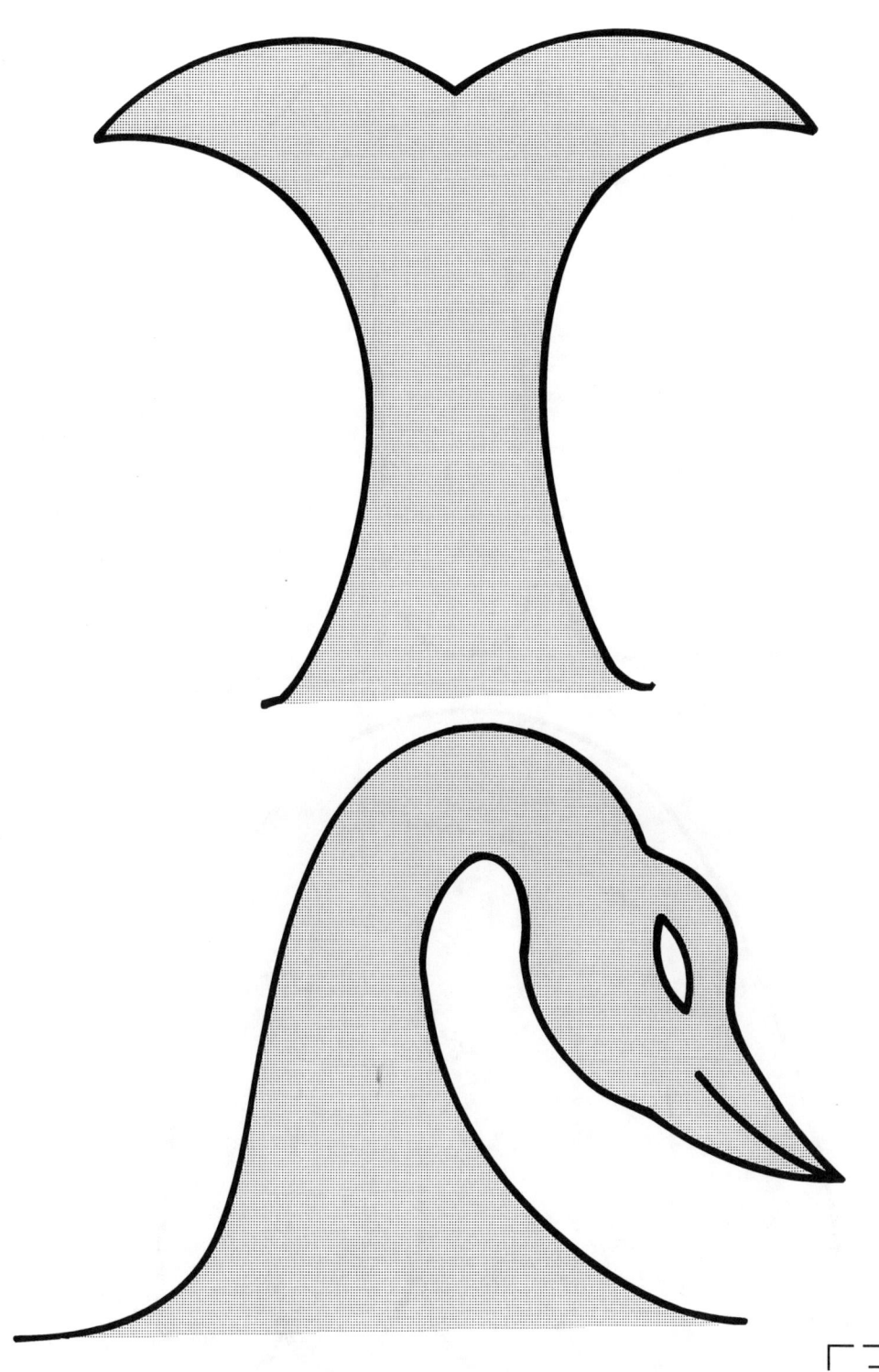

— See illustration on page 24 for reference. —

— NOTE —
Broken lines are shown to indicate relief and detail only, and should never be cut through!

Swan I

— *For detailed instructions on use of this stencil see pages 11-12.* —

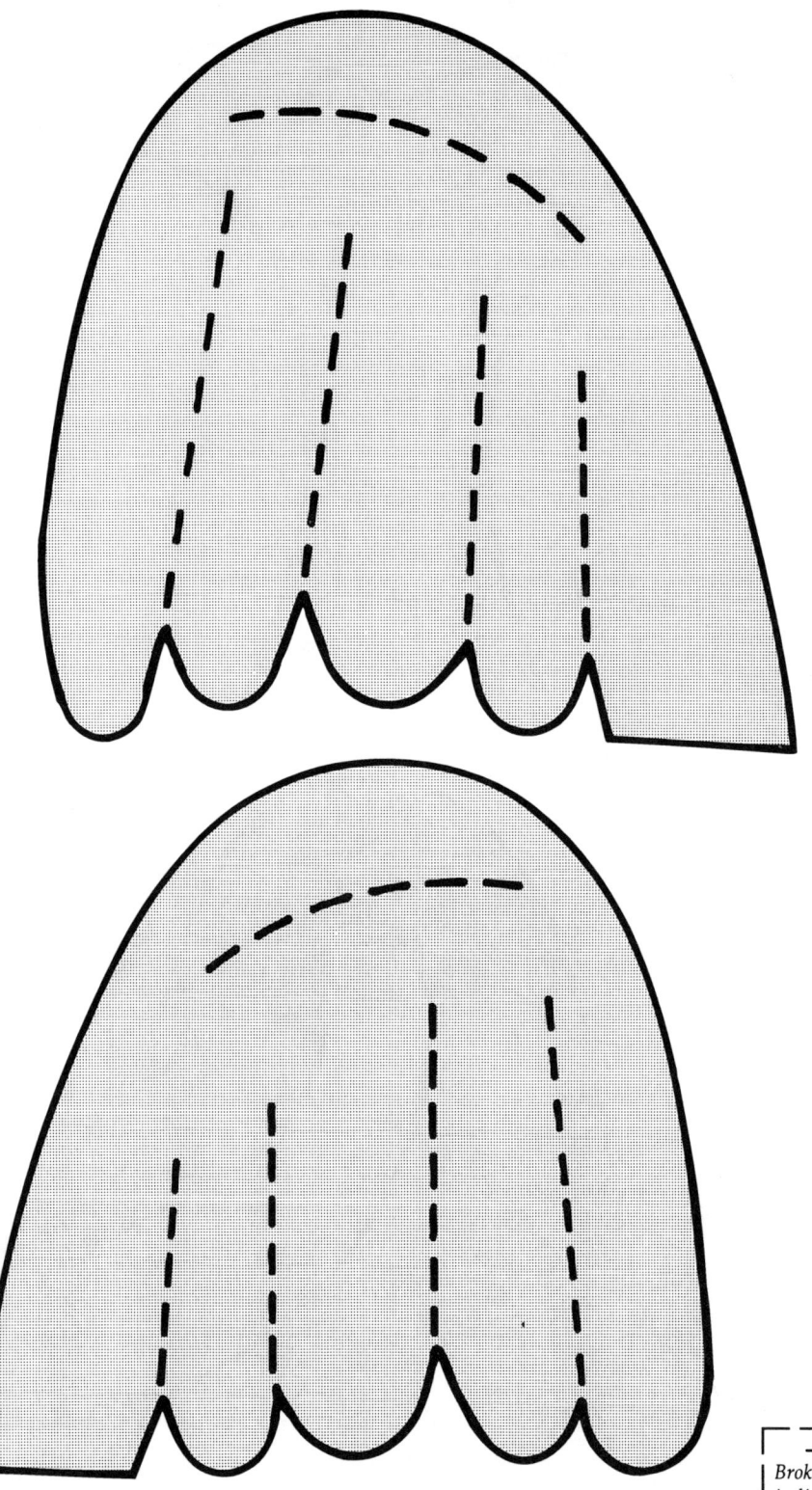

— *See illustration on page 24 for reference.* —

―― **NOTE** ――
Broken lines are shown to indicate relief and detail only, and should never be cut through!

Swan II

— Melon Required: Two Honeydews —

— *For detailed tool usage instructions, see pages 12-15-16-17.* —

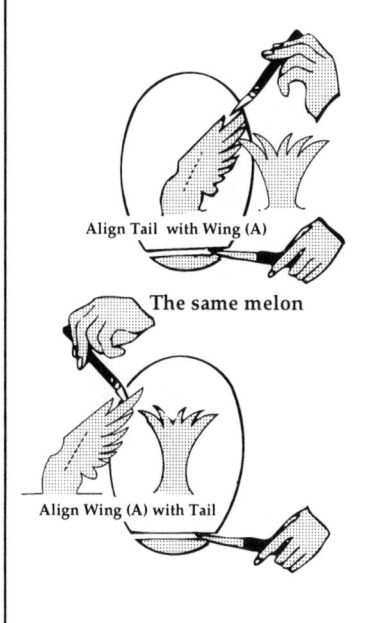

Align Tail with Wing (A)

The same melon

Align Wing (A) with Tail

1. Prepare first melon and stencils for carving using patterns, tape and X-acto knife. Lightly cut Swan II Wing (A) and tail (make sure you use the (A) Wing pattern and align properly designs on melon as shown) as described on page 12. Be sure to position pattern about 1-1/2" to 2" off the bottom of melon. Cut base as shown.

2. Using the Wing and Tail pattern you have traced as a guide, start to define part of the Swan II body itself. Add detail on broken lines as needed. Refer to illustration on page 24.

3. After you are satisfied with your carvings, using a spoon, clean out the inside of the melon.

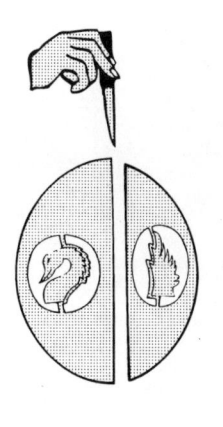

4. Using the 2nd melon, cut honeydew lengthwise into two sections, as shown. Remember, you will be carving the Swan II Wing (B) out of the large piece and using the small piece for carving the Swan Head.

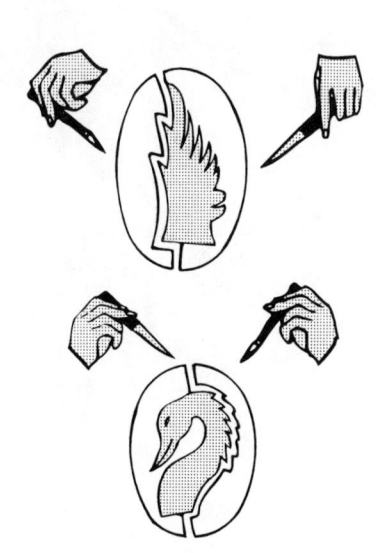

5. Prepare melon sections and stencils for carving using patterns, tape and X-acto knife. Trace Swan Wing and Swan Head on skin of melon pieces. Using the patterns you have traced as a guide and a paring knife define the Swan Wing and Head themselves. Refer to illustration on page 24.

6. Assemble carving with toothpicks, referring to illustration.

— *See finishing and decorating ideas on page 18.* —

Swan II

— *For detailed instructions on use of this stencil see pages 11-12.* —

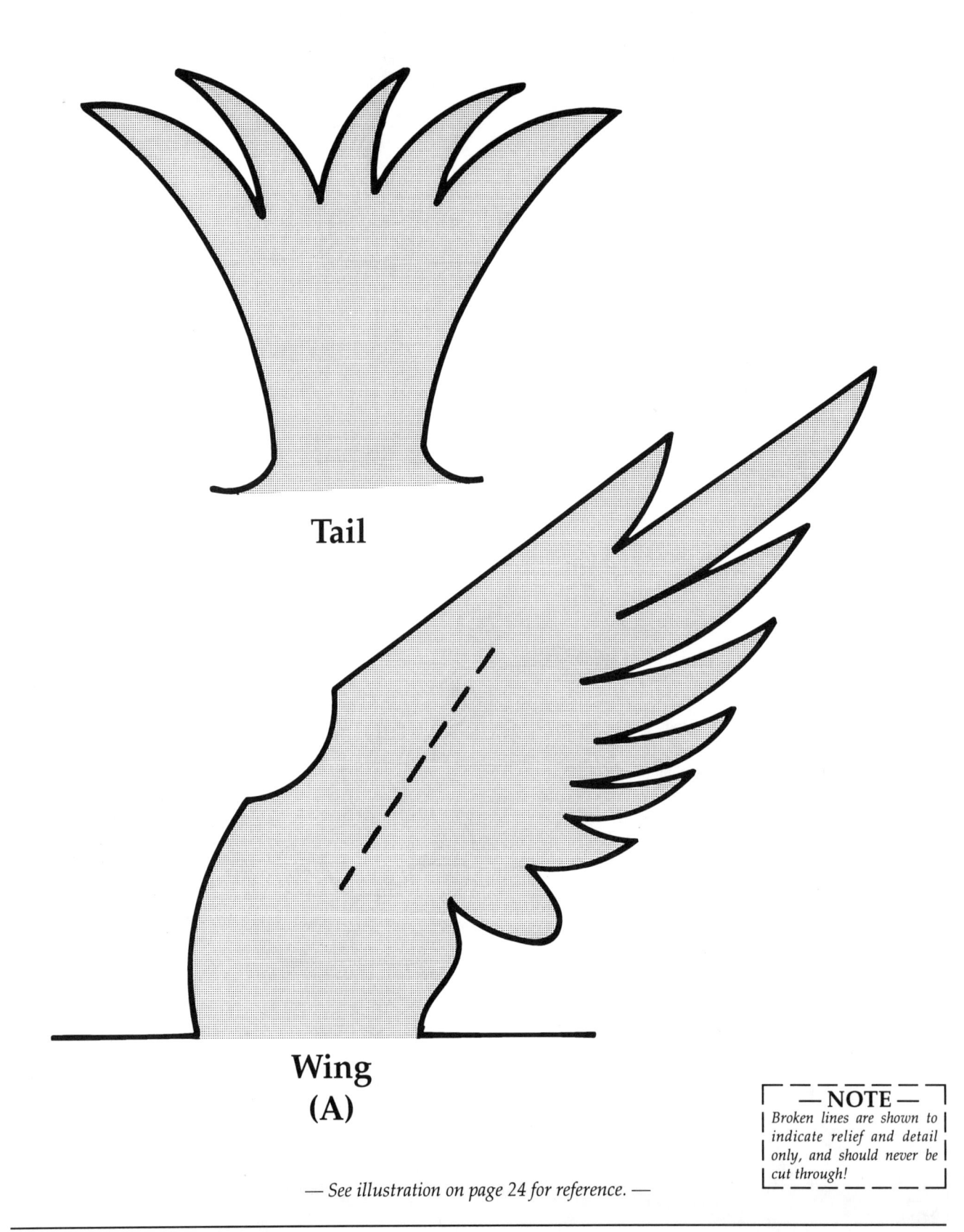

Tail

Wing (A)

— *See illustration on page 24 for reference.* —

— NOTE —
Broken lines are shown to indicate relief and detail only, and should never be cut through!

Swan II

— For detailed instructions on use of this stencil see pages 11-12. —

Wing (B)

— See illustration on page 24 for reference. —

— NOTE —
Broken lines are shown to indicate relief and detail only, and should never be cut through!

Notes

Notes

Letters, #s, & Marks

A B C D
E F G H
I J K L
M N O P
Q R S T

Letters, #s, & Marks

UVWX
YZ12
3456
7890
:;!?/""

Melon Recipes

Culinary Art

Boca Raton, Florida

Melon Recipes

While creating melon centerpieces, you will have melon and fruit left over. Here are some ideas that I have assembled for you to try and enjoy.

When preparing a dish, be creative and change recipes to satisfy your taste buds.

Use up extra melon pieces for you and your guests to enjoy. Entertainment is the taste of life.

"Balsamic" Dijon Herb Honeydew Salad

1	each honeydew, peeled and cut in medium chunks
1 1/2	cups red cabbage, shredded thin
1/2	cup red onion, diced fine
1/2	cup balsamic vinegar
1/4	cup olive oil or vegetable oil
2	tablespoons dijon mustard
1/4	cup chopped fresh basil
1/8	teaspoons black pepper, ground
2	tablespoons lemon juice, fresh
4	cups lettuce, romaine or iceberg, shredded thin
6	each strawberries, sliced

Peel and cut honeydew in medium chunks. In mixing bowl, add shredded red cabbage and diced red onion.

In blender, add Balsamic vinegar, olive oil, dijon mustard, fresh basil, black pepper and lemon juice. Blend for about 20 seconds.

Pour mixture over honeydew in mixing bowl and let stand, for a several hours, stir occasionally.

Serve on a bed of shredded lettuce and garnish with sliced strawberries.

Servings 3 to 4 people

Melon Recipes

Sesame Fried Melon with a Honey Lime Yogurt Sauce

Honey Lime Yogurt Sauce
1/2	cup plain yogurt
3	tablespoons honey
1/2	each lime (juice)
2	tablespoons mint, fresh chopped

Mix yogurt, honey, lime juice and mint thoroughly in a small bowl and place to the side to be used later.

8	melon slices 1/4 inch thick (large size pieces or add more small sections if that is all you have, no seeds).

Sesame Batter
1/2	cup flour, all purpose
1/4	cup milk
1	each egg white, whipped until fluffy (from large egg)
1	teaspoon sesame seeds
2	tablespoons honey
1	tablespoon soy sauce
1/4	teaspoon ginger powder
1/4	teaspoon baking powder

To taste black pepper, ground

In mixing bowl, add ingredients above, (except egg whites at this time) and mix thoroughly until batter is smooth, batter will be thick at this time.

Next, in small mixing bowl, whip egg white until fluffy. Add egg white to sesame batter and mix thoroughly, (sesame batter should have a pancake batter thickness).

Using a non-stick pan, heat over med-high heat, add oil. Dip slices of melon in batter and place in frying pan. Cook on each side for 2-3 minutes or until golden brown. Use spatula to gently turn over. Be careful!

On a plate, place 2 pieces of Sesame Fried Melon and spoon sauce over top, garnish with mint leaves and serve.

Serving 4 people

Melon Recipes

"Tropical" Melon Yogurt Soup

1/2	each cantaloupe, cut up and cleaned
6	each strawberries, cleaned no top
12	each blackberries
1/2	cup plain yogurt
3	tablespoons honey
1/2	each lime (juice)
2	tablespoons mint, fresh chopped
2	tablespoons rum or brandy (optional)

In a blender, add cantaloupe, strawberries, blackberries, honey and lime juice. Blend thoroughly for 1-2 minutes. Next, add yogurt, rum and blend 15- seconds. Serve in a bowl garnished with sliced strawberries and mint leaves.

Servings 4 people

— Mastering the Art of —
CARVING WATERMELON CENTERPIECES

An entertaining 110 pages on how to carve watermelon centerpieces. With the easy-to-follow instructions and templates, anyone can prepare party centerpieces. From fish to Christmas tree and birds, there is a carving for every occasion. A perfect gift for someone who entertains a lot. Or, for the woman who has everything

.ISBN 0-9628912-1-5

— Mastering the Art of —
CARVING MELON CENTERPIECES

Another entertaining 110 pages on how to carve melon centerpieces. Again with the easy-to-follow hand instructions and templates, anyone can carve melon party centerpieces. Over 30 melon design with illustrated instructions of how to carve honeydew and cantaloupe centerpieces. From fourth of July carvings to I Love You and holidays, there is a carving for every occasion.

.ISBN 0-9629277-1-6

• 112 PAGES • SOFT COVER •
RETAIL $9.95 EACH

• **Lonnie T. Lynch** •
– *Culinary Marketing* –

Publishing Venture

• **Lonnie T. Lynch** • **Culinary Marketing**
9850 Sandalfoot Boulevard, Suite 226
Boca Raton, FL 33428
(407) 852-0659

✂- - - - - - - ✂- - - - - - - ✂- - - - - - -

PLEASE SEND ME
___ WATER MELON BOOK AT $ 11.00 EACH*
___ MELON BOOK AT $ 11.00 EACH*
☐ CHECK   ☐ MONEY ORDER
   TOTAL ENCLOSED $ _____

• **Lonnie T. Lynch** •
– *Culinary Marketing* –

Publishing Venture

NAME_____

SHIPPING ADDRESS:_____

CITY/STATE/ZIP CODE_____

TELEPHONE: (   )_____

MAIL TO:
• Lonnie T. Lynch • Culinary Marketing
9850 Sandalfoot Boulevard, Suite 226
Boca Raton, FL 33428

* $1.05 SHIPPING HANDLING CHARGE ADD TO PRICE OF EACH BOOK